DOCUMENTA MISSIONALIA - 13

(STUDIA MISSIONALIA - DOCUMENTA ET OPERA)
FACULTAS MISSIOLOGICA - PONT. UNIVERSITÀS GREGORIANA

MEDITATION AS A PATH TO GOD-REALIZATION

A Study in the Spiritual Teachings of Swami Prabhavananda and his Assessment of Christian Spirituality

CYRIAC MUPPATHYIL MCBS

UNIVERSITÀ GREGORIANA EDITRICE - ROMA - 1979

PUBLISHED WITH THE SUPPORT OF
MISSIONSWISSENSCHAFTLICHES INSTITUT MISSIO e.V.
D-5100 — AACHEN, W.-Germany.

This book by CYRIAC MUPPATHYIL MCBS, *Meditation as a Path to God-Realization*, was published with Ecclesiastical approval by the Gregorian University Press in Rome 1979

Associato all'Unione Stampa Periodica Italiana

PREFACE

This study on Meditation as a Path to God-realization is a modest attempt to understand the idea-forces behind Hindu meditation as interpreted by Swami Prabhavananda. A study in his spiritual teachings will surely reveal the precious contents of Hindu meditation.

An Indian Christian experience cannot disregard the salient features of Hindu meditation. The relative lack of study on Hindu-Christian meditation is an indication of the need for a new approach to Indian Christian thought.

Within the Indian Church there is now a growing concern for dialogue with Hinduism. The consensus that there can be no fruitful dialogue based on doctrines alone is also growing. A dialogue with Hinduism demands a clear notion of its cardinal point of spirituality, namely meditation. It is with this hope that the present study is undertaken.

Two general notes of information may be helpful. First, unless otherwise indicated, quotations from the Upaniṣads are cited from The Thirteen Principal Upanishads, *trans. Robert E. Hume (second revised edition, 1931); those from the Gītā are cited from the standard translation by W. Douglas P. Hill (second abridged edition, 1953); biblical quotations are from the* Revised Standard Version *(Catholic edition, 1966). Secondly, Sanskrit terms are given in italics with the exception of the following: Brahman, Ātman, Īśvara and Yoga.*

I wish to acknowledge and thank Father Joseph Moonnanappallil MCBS, my Superior General, whose interest and encouragement made it possible for me to pursue the doctoral study. I acknowledge also the kindness of the Holy See in providing me with a scholarship. I am grateful to the Diocese of Augsburg, West Germany, for the financial support in the publication of the thesis. Thanks are also given to the professors of the Institute of Spirituality at the Gregorian University, Rome. I express my special thanks to Rev. Emile

Belletty and Rev. Sr. Richelle Williams, SSND, who very kindly helped with the proof-reading.

Finally, I acknowledge here genuine and heartfelt gratitude to Father Mariasusai Dhavamony S.J., director of the thesis. His scholarly knowledge and personal concern encouraged me to study Indian spirituality. For this precious gift, I shall always be grateful.

TABLE OF CONTENTS

ABBREVIATIONS

Ātmabodha	Śrī Śaṁkara's *Ātmabodha,* trans. and ed. with Notes, Comments, and Introduction by Swami Nikhilananda (Madras, 1947).
Gospel	*The Gospel of Sri Ramakrishna,* trans. Swami Nikhilananda (Madras, 1974).
RP	Swami Prabhavananda, *Religion in Practice* (London, 1968).
SHI	Swami Prabhavananda, *The Spiritual Heritage of India* (California, 1969).
Song of God	*The Bhagavad-Gita: The Song of God,* trans. Swami Prabhavananda (Madras, 1969).
VC	*Viveka Chudamani,* E.T. = *Shankara's Crest-Jewel of Discrimination,* trans. Swami Prabhavananda (New York, 1970).
Vedāntasara	*Vedāntasara of Sadānanda,* trans. Swami Nikhilananda (Calcutta, 1968).

These abbreviations for the Upaniṣads are also given here below:

AU	Aitareya Upaniṣad
BU	Bṛhad-āraṇyaka Upaniṣad
CU	Chāndogya Upaniṣad
KU	Kaṭha Upaniṣad
Mā U	Māṇḍukya Upaniṣad
MU	Muṇḍaka Upaniṣad
SU	Śvetāśvatara Upaniṣad
TU	Taittirīa Upaniṣad

Abbreviations for other sacred scriptures of Hinduism:

BG	Bhagavad-Gītā
RV	Ṛg Veda
YS	Yoga-sūtra

TRANSLITERATION OF SANSKRIT ALPHABET

VOWELS

short	a	i	u	e	o	ṛ
long	ā	ī	ū	ai	au	ṝ
anusvāra	ṁ					
visarga	ḥ					

CONSONANTS

gutturals	k	kh	g	gh	n
palatals	c	ch	j	jh	ñ
cerebrals	ṭ	ṭh	ḍ	ḍh	ṇ
dentals	t	th	d	dh	n
labials	p	ph	b	bh	m
semi-vowels	y	r	l	v	
sibilants	s	as in *sun*			
	ś	palatal sibilant pronounced like the soft Russian *s*			
	ṣ	cerebral sibilant as in *shine*			
aspirate	h				

INTRODUCTION

A. Swami Prabhavananda's understanding of spiritual life

Swami Prabhavananda's teaching on meditation springs from his general understanding of spiritual life. Therefore if we are to understand his teaching on meditation we have to make, beforehand at least, a very general survey of his understanding of spiritual life. As a representative of Advaita he holds that man in his innate nature is divine and that the realization of the divinity of man is the ultimate goal of spiritual life.

1. *Man Divine*

It seems an apparent contradiction of daily experience to say that man is divine. But one of the major propositions of Advaita is that man, in his true nature, is God. At the very outset we would like to make an important observation. Swami Prabhavananda makes use of many terms to designate God. They are: God, Brahman, Absolute, Sat-cit-ānanda, Īśvara, the Real, Reality, Being, Supreme Being, Supreme Truth, Existence, Infinite, Imperishable, Eternal and the Lord. Seeing the variety of these expressions, a reader may ask himself whether Swami Prabhavananda uses them indiscriminately. This only shows the struggle of the human mind to express adequately the reality of God. Swami Prabhavananda uses different terms because he fears that one word alone is not expressive enough. We have scrutinized the third chapter of *The Spiritual Heritage of India,* a portion of his writings dealing with the philosophy of the Upaniṣads in which he is expected to give an authentic view on the subject. We found that he uses eight terms to denote God: Brahman (109 times), God (18 times), Infinite (10 times), Supreme Being (5 times), the Real and its noun form Reality (3 times), Existence (3 times), Being (2 times) and Lord (once). The two terms found very often in the rest of his writings, Absolute and Īśvara, are not found here. All these terms, he says, philosophically speaking designate God. In the ultimate spiritual experience they do not make any fundamental distinction.[1]

In our study we use chiefly four terms: Brahman, Absolute, God and Īśvara. Of these, Brahman and Absolute signify the ultimate transcendental Reality of the Advaita, while God and Īśvara correspond to the Creator, the Preserver and the Destroyer of the universe.

The statement 'man is divine' points to the mystery of human existence. Swami Prabhavananda inquires into the truth of this mystery. We shall epitomize his teaching on this point.[2]

The *ṛṣis* [3] observed the world around them. They saw that it was in a constant movement. Birth, growth and death caught their attention. They asked themselves, whether there was some reality that persists in spite of the changes? What is the ultimate ground of existence? They saw something that made the only exception to the continuous change. This they named Brahman.

In a second moment they began to look within. Even here they observed a continuous change: sensation, emotion, thought, appearing one after another like the waves of a shoreless sea. They asked themselves whether something persisted? What is the innermost self that is immortal? Again they saw a silent, constant witness. They called it Self (Ātman).

Now in a third moment of reflection, the sages found out that these two persisting realities are one and the same. Brahman, the transcendental principle, enters into man and exists in him as his very self. Advaita teaches that Brahman, the One without a second, is the self of every man. The mystery of man is thus unveiled. This is a tremendous discovery.[4]

Here arises a question: If every man is divine, if every man is, in the strictest sense, Brahman, why are we not conscious of it? Swami Prabhavananda answers that this is so because of our over-

---

[1] Cf. SWAMI PRABHAVANANDA, *Religion in Practice* (London, 1968), p. 131. Hereafter abbreviated as RP.

[2] Cf. ID., *The Spiritual Heritage of India: A Comprehensive Exposition of Indian Philosophy and Religion* (California, 1969², first published in 1963), pp. 41-60. Hereafter referred to as SHI.

[3] *Ṛṣis* are the seers or sages who are said to have received revelation of the Veda, the sacred wisdom. They form a special class of beings, superior to men and inferior to the gods.

[4] Cf. 'M': *The Gospel of Sri Ramakrishna,* trans. Swami Nikhilananda (Madras, 1974⁶), p. 356. Hereafter referred to as *Gospel.*

concern with the empirical life. We have to change the natural orientation of our consciousness, says KU 2.1:

> The better (*śreyas*) is one thing, and the pleasanter (*preyas*) quite another.
> Both these, of different aim, bind a person.
> Of these two, well is it for him who takes the better,
> He fails of his aim who chooses the pleasanter (KU 2.1).

Man has to choose constantly between the good and the pleasant. The wise examine both and prefer the good to the pleasant. We generally lead outward lives. To have a vision of the truth we have to shut our senses to external objects and turn our gaze inward.

The cause of all our anxieties, unhappiness, confusion and spiritual emptiness, lies in the misapprehension of the ego for our real self. It is like taking the shadow for the reality. According to Advaita the most important spiritual discipline is to cease identifying oneself with the body, mind and senses and to recognize one's true nature which is divine.

2. *Unfolding Man's Divinity*

Above we have seen that according to Advaita man's true nature is divine. We have also seen how the sages came to this conclusion. But the Upaniṣads do not teach merely a theory. Their teaching is orientated to practice. In the Kena Upaniṣad 13 (5) the Teacher instructs:

> If one have known [It] here, then here is truth.
> If one have known [It] not here, great is the destruction (*vinaṣṭi*).
> Discerning [It] in every single being, the wise,
> On departing from this world, become immortal.

The man who realizes Brahman while he still lives is blessed; he who does not realize Brahman suffers his greatest loss. According to Swami Prabhavananda realization of our true nature is the only goal of our life and it must be achieved here and now. If we fail to do this, our life is in vain.[5]

Kena Upaniṣad begins with a few questions put by the disciple:

> By whom impelled soars forth the mind projected?

---

[5] Cf. Swami Prabhavananda, SHI, p. 62.

By whom enjoined goes forth the earliest breathing?
By whom impelled this speech do people utter?
The eye, the ear — what god, pray, them enjoineth?
(Kena U 1)

And the following verse contains the answers to his questions:

That which is the hearing of the ear, the thought of the mind,
The voice of speech, as also the breathing of the breath,
And the sight of the eye! Past these escaping, the wise,
On departing from this world, become immortal (Kena U 2).

The one who recognizes Brahman behind the ear, the mind, speech, breath and eye becomes immortal. Brahman is the eternal principle abiding in man as his inner Self. Man's primary duty is to realize, experience, enter into union with It.

According to Swami Prabhavananda the divinity of man is not an acquisition. It is remarkable that he uses terms such as realization, unfolding and awareness. From Śaṁkara to Swami Vivekananda, whom he considers the great interpreters of Advaita, teachers are emphatic on this point. They taught that to unfold the divinity already existing within is the end of evolution and goal of life. We shall conclude with the words of Swami Prabhavananda:

> The illumined seer does not merely know Brahman; he is Brahman, he is Existence, he is Knowledge. Absolute freedom is not something to be attained, absolute knowledge is not something to be won, Brahman is not something to be found anew ... The positive fact, our real nature, eternally exists. We are Brahman ...[6]

B. General outline and method of the study

Meditation as a Path to God-realization is a study in the teachings of Swami Prabhavananda on meditation. He is a noted commentator of Hindu scriptures. In his works he has consistently stressed the practice of meditation as a way to the experience of God. In this study we propose to present his teachings on meditation.

This study consists of six chapters. Each of the first four chapters highlights one aspect of Hindu meditation. They discuss respectively the meaning, forms, techniques and effects of meditation. The fifth chapter comments on Swami Prabhavananda's understanding

---

[6] *Ibid.*, p. 295.

of Christian meditation. The sixth chapter is an evaluation and conclusion, in which after examining the merits and demerits of Swami Prabhavananda's interpretation of meditation, we shall survey the principles for a Christian integration of Hindu meditation. We shall end the study, presenting meditation as a meeting-point for Hindu-Christian dialogue.

In the course of this study we shall follow a method of analysis and interpretation. This method shall have three phases: (1) Swami Prabhavananda's works. We shall carefully select those passages in his writings where he develops his idea of meditation. We shall analyse the principal texts on meditation. (2) To understand Swami Prabhavananda it is not enough to study his works alone. His spiritual teachings are derived from the sacred books of Hinduism, especially the Upaniṣads, the Bhagavad-Gītā and the Yoga-sūtra. Therefore, we shall have to analyse and interpret these sources themselves; however, not in a historical way but only as interpreted by him. (3) Swami Prabhavananda is a representative of neo-Hinduism and as a monk of the Ramakrishna Order has been inspired by the neo-Vedāntic movement. Hence, we shall have to interpret him in the light of neo-Hinduism rather than that of classical Hinduism.

CHAPTER I

THE MEANING OF MEDITATION

A. A GENERAL INTRODUCTION TO THE CHAPTER

Hinduism develops the idea of *mārga* (way, path), comparing man to a wayfarer. Is not spiritual life a journey in search of God? To follow the right path makes the journey pleasant and the goal secure. Thus in the course of time Hinduism has recognized three principal paths: *Karma mārga, Jñāna mārga,* and *Bhakti mārga.* Swami Prabhavananda adds the fourth, *Rāja mārga.* But all these four paths have the same destination. When the destination is arrived at, the paths become as if one.[1]

Descriptions of the different paths are found even in the earliest Hindu scriptures. One of the paths to enlightenment is *Karma mārga.* It is the path of right action. The Gītā exhorts the Karma yogi to be engaged in the service of God in all men, without desiring the fruit of action (BG 4.18). "... you must perform every action sacramentally, and be free from all attachment to results." [2]

Jñāna mārga is the path of union with God through true knowledge of God. It is an intellectual exercise of right discrimination. When all transitory phenomena are discarded, just as husk is separated from rice, the seeker sees God alone.

Bhakti mārga or the path of realization through love is the 'whole-souled devotion' to God.[3] As devotion grows, a transformation of the devotee takes place. In the culmination the devotee surrenders himself to God totally and unconditionally.

Rāja mārga, the royal path, is the approach to God through intense practice of meditation. According to Swami Prabhavananda

---

1 Cf. SWAMI PRABHAVANANDA, *Narada's Way of Divine Love,* trans. with a commentary on *Nārada Bhakti-sūtra* (California, 1971), pp. 67-68.

2 SWAMI PRABHAVANANDA and CHRISTOPHER ISHERWOOD, trs., *Bhagavad-Gita: The Song of God* (Madras, 1969), p. 100. Hereafter referred to as *Song of God.*

3 Cf. SWAMI PRABHAVANANDA, SHI, p. 128.

it is the technical name for the practice of meditation.[4] He even calls it "the yoga of meditation" since it stresses the value of formal, scientific meditation.[5]

Swami Prabhavananda admits the difficulty in defining this path, in so far as, in a sense, it includes all the other paths and at the same time remains distinct from them all including the *jñāna mārga.*[6] For it deals with mind and its powers, aiming at removing all mental obstructions and gaining the power of concentration. A concentrated mind, teaches *rāja mārga,* penetrates the true nature of the Self, a knowledge which is apt to shake off the worldly bondages and secure final liberation.

These are the more important paths to spiritual enlightenment prescribed by the sages. Our point is that all these paths have an orientation to meditation. Swami Prabhavananda expresses this by saying: "... meditation is to be practised as a discipline no matter which path the aspirant may follow." [7] This is more evident from his following text:

> Meditation is the very centre and heart of spiritual life. It matters not whether you are a follower of the path of Karma, or of devotion or knowledge, whether you are a Christian or a Buddhist or a Hindu, sooner or later you have to practise meditation; there is no other way. You may begin in divergent ways according to your beliefs and temperament, but as you proceed, as you approach the centre and heart of religion and religious practice, you come to that centre which is called meditation.[8]

It forms the thread that runs through the different paths connecting them as a whole.[9] Then, he continues:

> whatever path the spiritual aspirant chiefly follows, ... meditation is the most important aspect of his spiritual life. Somehow or other he must keep his mind fixed on God.[10]

---

[4] Cf. *ibid.*, p. 127.

[5] Cf. SWAMI PRABHAVANANDA, *How to know God: The Yoga Aphorisms of Patañjali* (A Mentor Book, New York, 1969), II.45. To facilitate references within our study we shall refer to this work as SWAMI PRABHAVANANDA on *Yoga-sūtra.*

[6] Cf. *ibid.*

[7] ID., *Narada's Way of Divine Love,* p. 68; cf. also JEAN HERBERT, *Spiritualité Hindoue* (Paris, 1947²), p. 363.

[8] SWAMI PRABHAVANANDA, "The Yoga of Meditation," in: *Vedanta for the Western World* (London, 1951, first published in 1948) ed. Christopher Isherwood, p. 80.

[9] Cf. SWAMI PRABHAVANANDA, SHI, p. 99.

[10] *Ibid.*, p. 348.

The above considerations will, we hope, serve to throw some light on the importance of meditation in Swami Prabhavananda's understanding of spiritual life. In the following pages we shall try to see the meaning he gives to the spiritual discipline of meditation.

B. Two types of spiritual disciplines

It has already been made clear that the goal of human life is the realization of Brahman. Hence it should be the ultimate concern of man. But are there any means to achieve this goal? The Upaniṣads prescribe two fundamental means. They are:

1. The moral discipline
2. The practice of meditation

1. *The Moral Discipline*

The Kaṭha Upaniṣad 3.3-9 gives the parable of the chariot. The Self is compared to the owner of the chariot (*rathin*) and the body (*śarīram*) to the chariot (*ratha*). Intellect (*buddhi, vijñāna*) is the charioteer (*sārathi*). The mind (*manaḥ*) controls the senses (*indriyāṇi*) which are said to be the horses running along the roads of sense objects. He alone reaches the end of the journey — which is Brahman — who keeps his senses under control. It is disastrous to be led by unbridled horses. In fact nothing is more dangerous to a man than his own uncontrolled mind.

Therefore certain moral disciplines are required of the seeker. The Taittirīya Upaniṣad enters somewhat more fully into details of conduct:

> Speak the truth.
> Practise virtue (*dharma*).
> Neglect not study [of the Vedas].
> Having brought an acceptable gift to the teacher, cut not off the line of progeny.
> One should not be negligent of truth.
> One should not be negligent of virtue.
> One should not be negligent of welfare.
> One should not be negligent of prosperity.
> One should not be negligent of study and teaching.
> One should not be negligent of duties to the gods and to the fathers.
> Be one to whom a mother is as a god.
> Be one to whom a father is as a god.

> Be one to whom a teacher is as a god.
> Be one to whom a guest is as a god.
> Those acts which are irreproachable should be practised, and no others.
> Those things which among us are good deeds should be revered by you, and no others (TU 1.11 passim).

But the perfect ideal of moral life taught in the Upaniṣads is to transcend both good and evil. According to the Muṇḍaka Upaniṣad 3.1.3 a knower of Brahman shakes off good and evil. No lamp is needed in the sunlight. When the experience of God is there, there is no more place for moral laws. That is why the Hindu mystics speak of transcending the ethical life. As taught by the sage Yājñavalkya:

> He is not followed by good, he is not followed by evil, for then he has passed beyond all sorrows of the heart (BU 4.3.22).
> He does not become greater by good action or inferior by bad action (BU 4.4.22).
> Him [who knows this] these two do not overcome — neither the thought "Hence I did wrong," nor the thought "Hence I did right." Verily, he overcomes them both. What he has done and what he has not done do not affect him (BU 4.4.22).
> This eternal greatness of a Brahman
> is not increased by deeds (*karman*) nor diminished.
> One should be familiar with it. By knowing it,
> One is not stained by evil action (BU 4.4.23).

This is not to say that one does evil with immunity. On the contrary, it means that one transcends the realm of morality and is practically incapable of doing evil. Swami Prabhavananda tries to explain the ideal of ethical life as taught by the Hindu sages in the following way:

> There have been scholars in the West who have brought against Hindu philosophy the charge that ethics play no important part in the religion of India; whereas, on the contrary, the Hindu philosophers and mystics clearly state that, in order to have the transcendental experience of the Reality, though it is necessary to go beyond both good and evil, beyond ethics, moral life is the very foundation of spiritual life. Nevertheless, we must rise above this foundation. This does not mean that we become unmoral. Just as a flower gives out fragrance without any consciousness of doing so, but because it is fragrant by its very nature, in the same way our natures must become such that we do what is good and moral without any consciousness of being good and moral; we

become moral because holiness has become a part of our very nature. This is what is meant by transcending ethical life.[11]

The above mentioned moral disciplines make the heart of the spiritual aspirant pure. Purity of heart is a necessary condition to enter into the life of the spirit. With a pure heart, the spiritual aspirant can now begin practising his meditation.

2. *The Practice of Meditation*

The Indo-Aryans showed great interest in a practice called meditation with the purpose of developing the inner faculties of man. Accordingly they conceived the human body as divided into different layers. The physical body (*sthūla śarīra*) covers the subtle body (*sūkṣma śarīra*). There is also a third called the causal body (*kāraṇa śarīra*). As the physical body needs food for its strength and growth, as the subtle body needs food for the mind and intellect, such as art, music and cultural activities, so too the causal body needs favourable conditions for its strength and growth. Love of God, devotion to God and meditation on God create the favourable atmosphere.

What Swami Prabhavananda thinks about meditation tells us more emphatically about its role in reaching God. It is considered to be the highest of all spiritual disciplines. As an approach to the divine goal, meditation is a vital means of success in spiritual life. M. Dhavamony clearly expresses:

> ... meditation, consisting of spiritual acts of knowledge and love of the divine, is the means preferred by the Indians to enter more deeply into the sphere of the sacred. It is no exaggeration to say that meditation ... is the method that is commonly used and most highly valued among the religious Hindus.[12]

In the same text he continues to observe that "meditation is the heartbeat of the Hindu religious practices ..." [13] and that "deeper religious insight comes mainly through meditation ..." [14]

This opinion is supported by the vast body of Hindu literature.

---

[11] SWAMI PRABHAVANANDA, "The Yoga of Meditation," in: *Vedanta for the Western World,* p. 83.

[12] M. DHAVAMONY, "Hindu meditation and Christian evaluation of it," in: *Secretariatus pro non Christianis Bulletin,* 23-24 (1973) 103.

[13] *Ibid.,* 104.

[14] *Ibid.,* 103.

According to the Maitrī Upaniṣad 4.4 "... by knowledge (*vidyā*), by austerity (*tapas*), and by meditation (*cintā*) Brahman is apprehended." The Bṛhad-āraṇyaka Upaniṣad 3.5.1 teaches that through silent meditation one becomes a knower of Brahman (*Brāhmaṇa*). Such a knower of Brahman becomes verily Brahman (MU 3.2.9). He is no more an ordinary man. The Śvetāśvatara Upaniṣad formulates:

> This has been sung as the supreme Brahma.
> In it there is a triad. It is the firm support, the Imperishable.
> By knowing what is therein, Brahma-knowers
> Become merged in Brahma, intent thereon, liberated from the womb [i. e. from rebirth]
> (SU 1.7).

The logic of the Upaniṣads seems to be as follows: the truth is Brahman.[15] Man is saved when he gains knowledge of this truth. Brahman gives its knowledge to a person who constantly thinks of It.[16] Therefore it is through meditation that Brahman is known and liberation obtained. In the *Prayers and Meditations* Swami Prabhavananda tackles the problem of knowing God. Giving a free translation of the Kaivalya Upaniṣad 5-9, he points out that there is no other way to liberation than meditation:

> Retire into solitude. Seat yourself on a clean spot and in erect posture, with the head and neck in a straight line ... Then enter the lotus of the heart, and there meditate on the presence of Brahman — the pure, the infinite, the blissful ... The seers meditate on him and reach the source of all beings, the witness of all ... He who knows him conquers death. There is no other way to liberation.[17]

We shall state here the Bhagavad-Gītā's teaching on the importance of meditation. Let us quote from the Gītā in order to better elucidate its view concerning the role of meditation in spiritual life. Swami Prabhavananda translates BG 6.3 as follows:

---

[15] In the Sanskrit version as well as in the standard translation of the Upaniṣads by E. Hume, the word used is Brahma. But It is different from Brahmā, one of the Divinities in the Hindu triad. The 'triad' in the above citation refers to the world, the individual self and the cosmic Self. In this study, except in quotations, we always use the word Brahman.

[16] Cf. SU 1.8; 2.14-15; 3.7,8,13; 4.14,16; 5.13,14; 6.13; BU 3.8.10; 4.4.14; Maitrī U 6.18.

[17] SWAMI PRABHAVANANDA and CLIVE JOHNSON, eds., *Prayers and Meditations: Compiled from the Scriptures of India* (California, 1967), No. 32.

> Let him who would climb
> In meditation
> To heights of the highest
> Union with Brahman.[18]

The Gītā, which has a long discourse on the physical conditions of meditation (BG 6.10-19), exhorts the aspirant to retire into solitude (v. 10), make his mind a single-point (v. 12), still his self, control his mind and think of Kṛṣṇa (v. 14); this is the way to peace and liberation (v. 16). Translating BG 8.8 as: "Make a habit of practising meditation and do not let your mind be distracted," [19] Swami Prabhavananda seems to think that meditation is the way to union with Brahman. Although there may be other means to reach God,[20] the one preferred by Kṛṣṇa is contained in the following verse of the Gītā:

> To that Ascetic, ceaselessly controlled, who ever ceaselessly with undivided thought remembers me, easy am I of access, son of Pṛitha (BG 8.14).

Intense meditation on God, to the exclusion of other objects, leads to the integration of the self and the spiritual vision of God. This teaching is taken up again in BG 9.22:

> To those men who think on me and worship me with undivided hearts, ever controlled, I bring the power to gain and guard.

The last chapter of the Gītā contains many instructions on meditation. Thus in 18.52 Kṛṣṇa asks the aspirant to practise meditation (*dhyāna-yoga*) constantly; in v. 57 he is told to give himself up in thought to Kṛṣṇa as the object of meditation and to be ever engaged in meditation on Him; in v. 58 Kṛṣṇa assures him of His help, saying that meditation on Him will save him from all dangers.

The discipline of meditation is prescribed not only to the specially qualified aspirants but to all seekers after the truth of God. The Bhāgavata Purāṇa time and again exhorts devotees to practise meditation unceasingly.[21] It compares meditation to a sword that cuts

---

18 Swami Prabhavananda, *Song of God*, p. 135.

19 *Ibid.*, p. 158.

20 BG 13.24: "Some through meditation see Self in self by self, others by the Sāṁkhya method; and others by the method of work." Here meditation, like knowledge and action, is only one of the ways, to see the Self in self.

21 Bhāgavata Purāṇa narrates an Indian folktale, according to which a cockroach, when attacked by a vramara-kita, becomes a vramara-kita. It always thinks of its enemy, in consequence of which it is transformed into its opponent. The lesson

the knots of ignorance and evil *karma*.[22] The sign of a wise man is that he never ceases to meditate.[23] This is also man's highest duty.[24] Reading Swami Prabhavananda's translation of the Bhāgavata Purāṇa, one is inclined to admit that meditation is the way to find God. "... that ye may meditate on me and find me within your own heart," [25] and "Even those who have not seen me and yet meditate on me, they also find me and attain to my being." [26]

Great interpreters of Advaita have always insisted on the importance of meditation in the spiritual unfolding. Śaṁkara, according to Swami Prabhavananda, is said to have taught that meditation, which has attained the height of direct perception, is spoken of in the scriptures as a means of liberation.[27] From the holy company of the disciples of Śrī Rāmakṛṣṇa he learnt that the knowledge of Brahman is directly attained only by one who practises meditation.[28] Thus Advaitins generally teach that without the practice of meditation no man can ever expect to reach the highest state of spiritual evolution.

We shall now sum up Swami Prabhavananda's ideas that pertain to this section as follows:

Advaita proposes a definite goal to man's life. It is the realization of Brahman. This realization becomes a reality with the knowledge of Brahman. A mere intellectual knowledge is inadequate to carry out this transformation. It should be an experiential knowledge, in which the truth of Brahman and the truth of one's own being are realized by the spiritual aspirant as one and the same. But where is the truth of our being? It is within ourselves. How can we find that which is within ourselves by looking outside? Here meditation comes to our aid as the principal means of investigation. It is the path of self-realization.

---

here is that the aspirant who unceasingly meditates on Brahman becomes ultimately Brahman. Cf. SWAMI PRABHAVANANDA, tr., *The Wisdom of God: Srimad Bhagavatam* (New York, 1968), p. 236.

22 Cf. *ibid.*, pp. 5,14. *Karma* or *Karman* refers to a chain of cause and effect, operating in the moral world as a consequence of an individual's actions in this and previous lives.

23 Cf. *ibid.*, pp. 228-229, 231.

24 Cf. *ibid.*, p. 159.

25 *Ibid.*, p. 206.

26 *Ibid.*, p. 207.

27 Cf. SWAMI PRABHAVANANDA, RP, p. 167.

28 Cf. ID., *The Eternal Companion: Spiritual Teachings of Swami Brahmananda* (Madras, 1971^5), pp. 32, 33, 46, 70, 270, 298, 336, 338.

C. The steps to meditation

The path to God has already been trodden by the sages of old. In the moments of deep spiritual illumination they realized the ultimate Reality. The eternal Truth revealed to them, as well as the method of the course they followed in their spiritual research, were transmitted from generation to generation. In the Bṛhadāraṇyaka Upaniṣad Yājñavalkya, after having explained to Maitreyī that every thing has value only in its relation to the Self, says:

> Lo, verily, it is the Soul (Ātman) that should be seen, that should be hearkened to, that should be thought on, that should be pondered on, O Maitreyī. Lo, verily, with the seeing of, with the hearkening to, with the thinking of, and with the understanding of the Soul, this world-all is known (BU 2.4.5).

In this text mention is made of three successive steps in reaching the Self,[29] i.e., hearing, reflection and meditation. Seeing of the Self is the consummation of the spiritual experience, while hearing, reflection and meditation on the Self lead to this direct perception of the Self. The three steps to the realization of God are:

1. *Śravaṇa*
2. *Manana*
3. *Nididhyāsana*

1. *Śravaṇa*

Śruti,[30] the sacred text, is the starting point of the spiritual research. The ultimate truth of God and Self is contained therein. Independent of the *śruti,* transcendental truths cannot be known. It is the seeker's duty to learn this ultimate truth in the Upaniṣads through study of the revealed texts.[31]

---

[29] In E. Hume's translation of the Upaniṣads 'Ātman' is rendered into English as 'Soul.' Today scholars agree that 'Self' is a more accurate translation. Except in quotations we always use the term Self. The self (with small *s*) indicates the individual self (ātman).

[30] The sacred texts of Hinduism are divided into: (1) *śruti* (2) *smṛti.* Of these the first is regarded as having originated in God Himself. It stands as an absolute authority.

[31] Cf. *Vedāntasara of Sadānanda,* tr. Swami Nikhilananda (Advaita Ashrama, Calcutta, 1968), Nos. 181-190. Hereafter the work shall be referred to as *Vedāntasara.*

Great stress is laid upon hearing the truth of Brahman from the lips of an illumined teacher. The Chāndogya Upaniṣad 4.9.3 declares that a teacher is indispensable: "for I have heard ... that the knowledge which has been learned from a teacher best helps one to attain this end." The Muṇḍaka Upaniṣad 1.2.12 asks the aspirant to approach his teacher with sacrificial fuel in hand, the ancient token with which a pupil approached a teacher. With the words 'I come to you, sir, as a pupil' (BU 6.2.7) he has to approach his teacher. A teacher is considered necessary to release the disciple from the bondage of ignorance, just as a man, blindfolded, and led away, and left in a strange place, needs someone to remove his bandages and show him the way home (CU 6.14.1-2). It is a rare privilege to learn about the Self from a master, says the Kaṭha Upaniṣad 2.7. The same Upaniṣad in 3.14 compares the seeker's way to a sharpened edge of a razor, difficult to tread, asking him to search for a guide. Confronted by problems of spiritual life, he seeks refuge in the person of the *guru,* who takes him by hand and helps him out of the confusion. The Chāndogya Upaniṣad records the story of the great sage, Nārada, approaching Sanatkumāra for instruction about Brahman (CU 7.1.1).[32] This is in conformity with the Hindu tradition which holds that spiritual knowledge is effective only when it is imparted through competent teachers.[33] "The ancient spiritual

[32] 'Teach me, sir!' — with these words Nārada came to Sanatkumāra. Gods like Indra were pupils of Praja-Pati (CU 8.7.2). Instances of this kind are numerous in the Upaniṣads. The fourth prapāṭhaka of the Chāndogya Upaniṣad tells two stories of discipleship: the one is how Jānaśruti got instruction from Raikva (4.1-3). The other is how Satyakāma went to Haridrumata Gautama saying: 'I will live the life of a student of sacred knowledge. I will become a pupil of yours, sir' (4.4.3). King Janaka was instructed by Yājñavalkya (BU 4.1-4). Although it was an anomaly that a Brahman should come to a Kṣatriya for instruction, Gārgya Bālāki requested Ajātaśatru: 'Let me come to you as a pupil' (BU 2.1.14). The same Bṛhad-āraṇyaka Upaniṣad, after having narrated the story of Śvetaketu (BU 6.2), gives the tradition of teachers (BU 6.3.7-12) with the conclusion: "One should not tell this to one who is not a son or to one who is not a pupil" (BU 6.3.12). Naciketas was taught by Death (Yama) about the need of a competent teacher:

He who by many is not obtainable even to hear of,
He whom many, even when hearing, know not —
Wonderful is the declarer, proficient the obtainer of Him!
Wonderful the knower, proficiently taught! (KU 2.7).

In the Taittirīya Upaniṣad 3.1 Bhṛgu Vāruṇi requests his father Varuṇa to teach him Brahman. The Kaivalya Upaniṣad 1ff speaks of Āśvalaya beseeching the Lord Brahmā for the knowledge of Brahman. While Pratardana Daivodāsi was taught by Indra (Kauṣītaki U 3.1ff), King Bṛihadratha was taught by Sākāyanya (Maitrī U 1.2-6.28). In the Praśna Upaniṣad sage Pippalāda is the honourable teacher (Praśna U 1.1ff).

[33] Swami Prabhavananda translates BG 4.34 as follows: "Those illuminated

wisdom of India has come down to the present time through an unbroken succession of teachers." [34] In the words of Śrī Rāmakṛṣṇa: "One understands the scriptures better by hearing them from the lips of the guru or of a holy man." [35]

The Muṇḍaka Upaniṣad 1.2.12 lays down some of the essential qualifications of a *guru.* They are commented on by Śaṁkara.[36] First of all, he must be thoroughly grounded in the Vedic knowledge. In order to awaken the disciple's spiritual consciousness, he must be filled with the wisdom of the sacred scriptures. He explains the scriptures, the spirit as well as the letter. Secondly, he must be established in Brahman (*brahma-niṣṭham*). He teaches by his life. The disciple sees in him a man of realization. He is endowed with the power, known as *śaktipāta,* to transfer his spiritual powers to a worthy disciple. This is symbolized in initiation (*dīkṣā*), during which he transmits spiritual power with the help of a name of God (*mantra*).

Having obtained from such an illumined spiritual guide the secret of Self, " whereby what has not been heard of becomes heard of, what has not been thought of becomes thought of, what has not been understood becomes understood " (CU 6.1.3), the aspirant is now prepared to follow the next step.

2. *Manana*

Knowledge of Brahman obtained from the revealed scriptures, with the help of the *guru,* is of supernatural character and as such takes us beyond the range of reason. However, it never contradicts reason. *Śravaṇa* does not mean that one should blindly accept what

---

souls who have realized the Truth will instruct you in the knowledge of Brahman, if you will prostrate yourself before them, question them and serve them as a disciple." SWAMI PRABHAVANANDA, *Song of God,* p. 120.

34 *Self-knowledge.* E. T. of Śaṁkara's *Ātmabodha* with Notes, Comments and Introduction by Swami Nikhilananda (Madras, 1947), p. 40. This was the custom in ancient India even if the pupil had already learnt the Veda in the family. See, for example, the final words to the departing disciple in CU 8.15.

35 *Gospel,* p. 431.

36 Cf. *Viveka Chudamani* = E. T. *Shankara's Crest-Jewel of Discrimination,* trs. Swami Prabhavananda and Christopher Isherwood (Mentor Book, New York, 1970), Nos. 35-44. Hereafter cited as VC. "A TEACHER is one who is deeply versed in the scriptures, pure, free from lust, a perfect knower of Brahman. He is upheld continually in Brahman ..." VC, No. 35. J. GONDA, *Change and Continuity in Indian Religion* (London, 1965), pp. 229-283, enumerates twenty-five qualities of a *guru.* Cf. also SWAMI PRABHAVANANDA, SHI, pp. 29, 147.

is being said. To understand the truth one has to make a thorough investigation into the scriptural statements, bringing out their inner significance. Hence there is justification for philosophical reflection in the approach to the spiritual goal.

In this connection Swami Prabhavananda treats the six systems of Indian philosophy[37] as *manana* or reflection on the truth of the sacred scriptures.[38] It provides a rational basis for the truth of Brahman. It is arguing with oneself in order to dispel remaining doubts. The disciple asks himself why the Upaniṣadic teaching alone is true? How is it that Brahman alone is real? What is the value of the phenomenal world? In this way, it takes away from the mind all doubts regarding the truth. Now the mind is completely drawn toward Brahman in such a way that it automatically enters into the subsequent stage of spiritual evolution which is *nididhyāsana.*

3. *Nididhyāsana*

With hearing and reflection the spiritual seeker has arrived at the intellectual conviction of the spiritual truth, but he should not stop there. The real test of conviction is to act accordingly. Scriptural truth, supported by reason, must finally be experienced in deep meditation. The old impressions (*viparīta-bhāvana*) are still there in a dormant state. These have to be completely eradicated. Here books are of no use. One has to transform the intellectual conviction into immediate experience. The experience of the phenomenal world is immediate, and in order to transcend it, another experience of the same order must be had. The truths heard from the sacred texts have bearing on life only to the extent they become spiritual perception (*darśana*). It is intuitive experience (*aparokṣa anubhūti*) alone which gives the final stamp. There is a certain degree of conviction in hearing and reflection: in the first a verbal conviction and in the second an intellectual conviction. But in meditation there is a merging of conviction into a direct intuition of the Absolute.

The goal of meditation is not mere knowledge; it aims at visualizing the truth of Brahman. For this purpose it fixes the mind on It in an intense manner. The illusory nature of the world begins to disappear. The example used by Śaṁkara is of gold which has

---

[37] The six systems of Indian philosophy are: the Vaiśesika of Kaṇāda, the Nyāya of Gotama, the Sāṁkhya of Kapila, the Yoga of Patañjali, the Mīmāṁsa of Jaimini and the Vedānta of Vyāsa.

[38] Cf. SWAMI PRABHAVANANDA, SHI, pp. 66 n. 4; 199, 208.

been refined in hot fire and purified of dross.[39] So also the mind is purified from all its impurities by means of constant thought of God. The value of meditation is recognized by Swami Prabhavananda when he says: "The surest means toward this realization or immediate perception of the truth of the Self and God is the habit of meditation." [40] It is the last step that opens the door to realization.[41]

We have briefly examined the triple approach to Brahma-realization. Here a word concerning their mutual relation would not be out of place:

1. The three steps are not three separate methods, independent of each other. Rather they are three methods of a single course. The three together lead to the realization of Brahman (BU 2.4.5; 4.5.6).

2. The three steps are mental activities. Hearing is a mental activity in so far as it brings the ascertainment that Brahman is the sole reality. Reflection is a mental operation which secures intellectual conviction. The same is true also of meditation, which is fixing the mind constantly on Brahman, producing the preliminary stage of Brahma-knowledge.

3. Their mutual relation is deep in the sense that hearing leads to reflection, which in turn leads to meditation.

4. The three steps have an ascending degree of value. As stated by Śaṁkara:

> It is a hundred times better to reflect on the truth of Brahman than merely to hear about it from the scriptures. And meditation is a hundred thousand times better than reflection.[42]

Before ending this article we must still make an assessment of the exact meaning of the terms *nididhyāsana, dhyāna* and *upāsanā,* three terms which are often loosely translated into English as meditation. This we intend to do with the hope of better understanding the meaning of meditation.

In his writings Swami Prabhavananda makes use of the term meditation to mean both *nididhyāsana* and *dhyāna.*[43] The problem

---

[39] Cf. VC, No. 367.

[40] SWAMI PRABHAVANANDA, *Vedic Religion and Philosophy* (Madras, 1950[5]), pp. 99-100.

[41] Cf. ID., RP, p. 117.

[42] VC, No. 364.

[43] Cf. SWAMI PRABHAVANANDA, *Yoga and Mysticism* (California, 1972), p. 23. He admits that meditation is not an entirely accurate translation of *dhyāna.*

arises mainly because such Sanskrit terms do not have exact English equivalents.

There are three types of spiritual aspirants: (1) *uttama adhikāri* or the most qualified seeker; (2) *madhyama adhikāri,* the second grade seeker; and (3) *adhama adhikāri,* the dull seeker. *Nididhyāsana,* being the direct approach to Brahman, can be practised only by the specially gifted seeker. For it is different from *dhyāna,* in so far as it is more like a process of knowledge. In the Bṛhadāraṇyaka Upaniṣad 2.4.5 and 4.5.6 we see that *nididhyāsana* is substituted by *vijñāna* (right apprehension). Here in this context *vijñāna* means: the means to an immediate intuition of Brahman. But *dhyāna* is an uninterrupted flow of thought usually upon a particular form of deity. True, both *vijñāna* and *dhyāna* are mental operations. An illustration is used to mark out the difference between the two. In front of an image of a deity, the knower has no option but to see it. In the case of a meditator, his will is the deciding factor. In other words, knowledge is determined by the nature of the thing known, whereas meditation depends on the knower's mind.

Strictly speaking, *nididhyāsana* is not meditation on the Self as Brahman, but the apprehension of the Self as Brahman. This is done by means of subtle discrimination. But Advaitins regard it as a special case of meditation. For right apprehension is finally followed by contemplation. Both in *nididhyāsana* and in *dhyāna* concentration is a significant factor — and for this reason they are often not distinguished one from another.

To say a word on *upāsanā,* which will be more closely dealt with in the next chapter, it is meditation with the help of a symbol, prescribed for the second grade spiritual seekers.

Having thus discussed the steps to meditation, we are now in a better position to understand the meaning of meditation.

D. The meaning of meditation

We have seen the importance of meditation in Swami Prabhavananda's idea of spiritual life. Here we intend to unfold the meaning of meditation in its various aspects.

The most significant meaning given to meditation by Swami Prabhavananda is that it is the personal experience of revelation. He interprets Śaṁkara as having taught: that regarding the truth of Brahman scriptures are not the only authority.[44] The scriptures contain the truth of Brahman, but each one should experience their contents for himself.

The authority of the scriptures comes from the fact that their truth can be verified. No sage ever claimed that these truths are revealed exclusively to him. Quoting Vāma-deva, a sage of the fourth book of the Ṛg Veda (RV iv.26.1), the Bṛhad-āraṇyaka Upaniṣad says:

> Verily, in the beginning this world was Brahma. It knew only itself (*ātmānam*): 'I am Brahma!' Therefore it became the All. Whoever of the gods became awakened to this, he indeed became it, likewise in the case of seers (*ṛṣi*), likewise in the case of man. Seeing this, indeed, the seer Vāmadeva began:
>
> I was Manu and the sun (*Sūrya*)!
>
> This is so now also. Whoever thus knows 'I am Brahma!' becomes this All; even the gods have not power to prevent his becoming thus, for he becomes their self (*ātman*) (BU 1.4.10).

Personal experience of the truth of God is the final proof. Swami Prabhavananda holds that the only proof for the existence of God is that He can be known and experienced.[45] One cannot be called spiritual until one has experienced the truth of God for oneself. Such personal experience of God is the heart of religion. Religion is neither an intellectual exercise nor a set of dogmas. It is the response of the total man. We come to the knowledge of God not through the subtlety of our intellect, but through personal experience. Therefore to experience God is the very essence of religion. If God remains a mere hypothesis, there is no religion at all. Intellectual belief is abstract, incapable of taking man to the sphere of the Divine. He criticizes Christianity for its lack of emphasis on this experience.[46]

Religious experience carries conviction within itself. For it is an immediate proof and an intuitional consciousness.[47] Śaṁkara considers it an ineffable experience, transforming our whole life and introducing us to the divine presence.[48] It is the unitive knowledge

---

44 Cf. Swami Prabhavananda, RP, p. 32.

45 Cf. Id., *Yoga and Mysticism,* p. 14.

46 Cf. *ibid.,* p. 13.

47 R. D. Ranade, *Vedanta the Culmination of Indian Thought.* Basu Mallik Lectures on Vedanta Philosophy in March 1929, Calcutta University (Bombay, 1970), p. 46: "Brahman is not an object of cognition (Avedya) but intuitional (Aparoksa-vyaharayogya)."

48 Cf. VC, Nos. 481-485.

of Brahman, taught by the Upaniṣads. Upaniṣadic knowledge is one with reality. To know Brahman is to become Brahman. Naciketas, having been instructed by the King of Death, was united with Brahman. The Narrator says that this is the case with anyone who has this knowledge.[49]

The revealed scriptures are the record of the spiritual experiences of the seers of truth. In the 'cave of the heart' (KU 3.1)[50] they meditated day and night.[51] In meditation their minds were illumined (MU 2.2.9-10) and Brahman was revealed to them (MU 3.1.8). In the experience of Brahman all their doubts disappear and "the knot of the heart is loosened" (MU 2.2.8). This experience is so real that the Upaniṣads even speak of 'seeing' Brahman (MU 3.1.3).

We have already stated that meditation is the personal experience of revelation. Here, a brief discussion on the Hindu idea of revelation becomes necessary in order to determine the meaning of meditation.

Hinduism teaches that its sarced texts contain the revelation of God. In the Bṛhad-āraṇyaka Upaniṣad they are said to have been breathed out by the Eternal:

> It is — as, from a fire laid with damp fuel, clouds of smoke separately issue forth, so, lo, verily, from this great Being (*bhūta*) has been breathed forth that which is Rig-Veda, Yajur-Veda, Sāma-Veda, [Hymns] of the Atharvans and Angirases, Legend (*itihāsa*), Ancient Lore (*Purāṇa*), Sciences (*vidyā*), Mystic Doctrines (*upaniṣad*), Verses (*śloka*), Aphorisms (*sūtra*), Explanations (*anuvyākhyāna*) and Commentaries (*vyākhyāna*). From it, indeed, are all these breathed forth (BU 2.4.10).

This idea is repeated later in the same Upaniṣad in 4.5.11 and forms part of the Hindu belief.[52] The sages are said to have heard and

---

49 Cf. KU 6.18. Other pertinent passages from the Upaniṣads are:
"He, verily, who knows that supreme Brahma, becomes very Brahma" (MU 3.2.9).
"Om! He who knows Brahma, attains the highest!" (TU 2.1).
"Being very Brahma, he goes to Brahma" (BU 4.4.6).

50 MU 3.1.7 "in the secret place of the heart."

51 Kena U 30 (5) "repeatedly."

52 The *śruti* was the heritage only of the 'twice-born.' That it was not communicated to the out-castes (*śūdra*) from the fear that it would be defiled, together with the scrupulous provisions to preserve the letter of the text in such a way that it has to be committed to memory is, perhaps, an indication that the Hindus believed in the sacred character of it. Cf. A. S. Geden, "Inspiration (Hindu)," in: J. Hastings' *Encyclopaedia of Religion and Ethics* vol. VII (Edinburgh T. & T. Clark, 1914), p. 353.

seen the Veda[53] which they communicated to men. Swami Prabhavananda says that Hinduism is founded on supernatural revelation; the Hindus believe that Vedic scriptures record revealed truths. He says:

> ... the orthodox Hindu regards the Vedas as his highest written authority. Any subsequent scripture, if he is to regard it as valid, must be in agreement with them: it may expand upon them, it may develop them, and still be recognized, but it must not contradict them. They are to him, as nearly as any human document can be, the expression of divine truth.[54]

He also says that the Vedas stand for Divine Truth and that they are the perfect Knowledge which is God. They claim to be divine in origin (*apauruṣeya* = not belonging to man). They existed before the creation of mankind.[55] The whole universe is said to have been made out of the knowledge of the Vedas.

Having affirmed that the Vedas are the final and infallible authority of the truth of God, Swami Prabhavananda goes on to explain his idea of revelation. According to him the truth of revelation is something which is otherwise unknown and unknowable.[56] What is hidden to human eyes is opened up by God. There is a four-fold revelation. The first is a partial revelation of Brahman in all forms of existence, since Brahman is Its own light (*svaprakāśa*). The second is the main type of revelation: at the beginning of each cosmic cycle the Lord (Īśvara) promulgates the Veda which contains the final truth about Brahman. When people forget this eternal truth about salvation, an *avatār* appears in order to reveal the eternal wisdom, which has been forgotten, but which has been contained in the Veda. This is the third kind of revelation. The fourth and final kind of revelation comes through the direct personal experience of Brahman, which arises through meditation on the

---

53 Note the difference between the Veda which is sacred knowledge, contained in the sacred scriptures which form the undeniable authority in rligious matters; and the Vedas which stand for the four Vedas such as Ṛg Veda, Yajur Veda, Sāma Veda and Atharva Veda.

54 SWAMI PRABHAVANANDA, tr., *The Upanishads: Breath of the Eternal.* The principal texts selected and translated from the original Sanskrit (Mentor Book, New York, 1957), p. xi.

55 M. Dhavamony notes that the Veda is not eternal in the sense in which Brahman is, granted that it is beginningless and everlasting. Cf. M. DHAVAMONY, "Revelation in Hinduism," in: *Studia Missionalia,* 20 (1971) 178.

56 Cf. SWAMI PRABHAVANANDA, SHI, p. 16.

sacred texts. To this last kind he ascribes great importance. For according to him it is transcendental knowledge or superconscious vision.[57] Moreover, he says that although scriptures are the revelations given to the sages, any one who develops superconscious power can receive revelation.[58]

Christian theologians would doubt whether this is strictly revelation at all. M. Dhavamony, who holds that the holy scriptures of Hinduism are in the true sense not revealed because they contain human efforts aided by God to realize Him, says:

> Revelation is however not only manifestation or information of certain truths or doctrines, even when they might be divine, but also divine self-opening which demonstrates God's intention and deeds with regard to man; thus beside God's words God's deeds also will be seen as revealing.[59]

He continues to say that Hinduism has changed the meaning of the idea of revelation into an empirical one, that is to say, it accepts as "revealed" the contents of a book or the character of a sage, but not the fact that God has really communicated them.[60]

Finally, Swami Prabhavananda compares the attitude of a Hindu and of a Christian towards their sacred scriptures.[61] He claims that Vedic revelation is superior to Christian revelation which, he says, is accepted in faith; nobody seriously thinks of verifying it in personal experience. Thus according to him the dynamism of religious experience is lacking in the Christian idea of revelation. This assertion too is questionable. Whereas, he agrees with the contents of the scripture but believes in their efficacy on the condition that he realized them for himself; the Christian, with free will, surrenders

---

57 Cf. Id., RP, p. 71.

58 Cf. *ibid.*, p. 72. On page 170 he says:
"These are revealed truths. They have been directly and immediately experienced by the seers and sages, within the depths of their own souls. Such truths are, of course, universal; and can be realized by every one of us who is ready to make the effort to do so."

59 M. Dhavamony, „Die Einstellung des christlichen Gottesdienstes zu den heiligen Schriften des Hinduismus," in: *Concilium,* 12 (1976) 80: „Offenbarung ist aber nicht nur Kundgebung oder Mitteilung gewisser Wahrheiten oder Lehren, auch wenn sie göttlich sein mögen, sondern göttliche Selbsteröffnung, die Gottes Absicht und Handeln mit dem Menschen anzeigt; neben Gottes Worten werden somit auch Gottes Taten als offenbarend angesehen."

60 Cf. *ibid.*

61 Cf. Swami Prabhavananda, SHI, p. 25.

totally to God's Word in the Bible. A greater dynamism than this is difficult to be found in the Hindu attitude.

Meditation imparts knowledge of Brahman. It is difficult to know Brahman. Following the path of meditation the wise man knows It (KU 2.12). Negatively, one cannot know Brahman, if one does not meditate (KU 2.24). Brahman is revealed in the heart through the insight obtained in meditation (KU 3.12). The truth of Brahman is not grasped by the senses, but by meditation (MU 3. 1.8). Absorbed in meditation, the seeker sees Brahman within himself and all things in It (BU 4.4.23).

Meditation trains the mind for spiritual experience. Sinking oneself in meditation, the yogi 'sees' Brahman. In worshipful contemplation (*samyak* + *ārādhana* = *samrādhana*) there comes a direct awareness of Brahman (*Brahmadarśanam*). Its vision becomes a fact of personal experience, where the human heart achieves its fulfilment. It is an inner experience in which man becomes what his spiritual life demands of him. Śrī Rāmakṛṣṇa told a parable of a salt doll that went to measure the depth of the ocean and tell it to others. No sooner did it get into the water than it dissolved.[62] Such is the spiritual exercise of meditation, which is the losing of oneself in the ocean of infinitude.

The sacred scriptures make use of different illustrations to explain the meaning of meditation. The Gītā employs the simile of the flame of a candle protected in a windless place. Swami Prabhavananda translates BG 6.18-19 as follows:

> When can a man be said to have achieved union with Brahman? When his mind is under perfect control and freed from all desires, so that he becomes absorbed in the Atman, and nothing else. "The light of a lamp does not flicker in a windless place": that is the simile which describes a Yogi of one-pointed mind, who meditates upon the Atman.[63]

The meditant absorbs his mind and intellect in the thought of God. The thought on God is so intense that it is single and undisturbed. Like an unbroken current, it fixes the mind steadily on God. It is to be noted that Hindu meditation is not a succession of many thoughts on the same subject. Hence a man is really meditating when his mind is freed from all other thoughts and is wholly focused on the object of his concentration.

---

[62] Cf. *Gospel,* p. 29.

[63] SWAMI PRABHAVANANDA, *Song of God,* p. 140.

The simile used by Rāmānuja, the twelfth-century exponent of qualified non-dualism (Viśiṣṭādvaita), is also significant. He compares meditation to the uninterrupted flow of oil from one vessel to another, in such a way that the successive drops form a continuous line:

> 'Meditation' means steady remembrance, i. e. a continuity of steady remembrance, uninterrupted like the flow of oil; in agreement with the scriptural passage which declares steady remembrance to be the means of release, 'on the attainment of remembrance all the ties are loosened' ... knowledge repeated more than once (i.e. meditation) is determined to be the means of Release.[64]

Śaṁkara uses the illustration of a devoted wife lost in the thought of her husband.[65] She steadily remembers him with longing. Such constant remembrance of God purifies the mind from all bondages and makes the heart worthy of God. Hindu spiritual teachers say that the mind is like a clean cloth which takes the colour of the dye in which it is dipped.[66] The reason is that the mind has a tendency to yield to a thought with which it was occupied for a long time. When the mind is constant in contemplation on God, He is revealed to it.

Let us note here that a confusion may arise whether the method of meditation spoken of in the preceding pages is yogic or Advaitic.

Advaita and the Yoga system of Patañjali share between them much with regard to meditation. According to both of them liberation is the ultimate aim, reached in the realization of the Self in one case, and in the isolation of the Spirit from Nature in the other. Advaita calls this state undifferentiated enstasis (*nirvikalpa samādhi*) and Yoga superconscious enstasis (*asamprajñāta samādhi*).[67] This much they are agreed upon. But they differ in their views regarding the realization of the Self, superconscious state and liberation itself. This is because they follow two different philosophies.

According to Advaita, Brahman is the only Reality, while everything else is only Its apparent modification (*vivarta*). Patañjali's Yoga system, on the other hand, admits two basic principles: Spirit

---

64 *Śrī Bhāṣya* I.1.1. The citation is taken from *The Vedānta-Sūtras with the commentary of Rāmānuja,* trans. George Thibaut (Oxford, 1904). The work is vol. XLVIII of *The Sacred Books of the East,* ed. F. Max Müller.

65 Cf. *Śaṁkara Bhāṣya on the Vedānta Sūtras* IV.i.8.

66 Cf. MONKS OF THE RAMAKRISHNA ORDER, *Meditation* (London, 1972), pp. 1-2.

67 A state of perfect control of mind as unrelated to any object. It is different from conscious enstasis which is a state of perfect concentration of mind.

(*puruṣa*) and Nature (*prakṛti*).[68] It holds that the phenomenal world is the real transformation (*pariṇāma*) of Nature.

Nature produces twenty-four categories of objects, of which pure mind-stuff (*mahat*) is the most important. Spirit, when associated with the mind-stuff, is erroneously identified with the latter. In Advaita there is a parallel thought; it too speaks of the erroneous identification of the Self with the non-self. To differentiate the Spirit from the mind-stuff and the Self from the non-self, both Yoga and Advaita employ the practice of meditation. Advaita accepts the eightfold practical course of Yoga. We should, however, bear in mind that the two systems differ in their methods of meditation.

The Yogic method of meditation is predominently isolationistic. For the realization of the Spirit, it sets the ideal of complete isolation or aloofness of Spirit from Nature in general and from the mind-stuff in particular. Advaita also speaks of discrimination between the Real and the unreal, the Self and the non-self. But here it is with a positive purpose of realizing Brahman as one's own inmost self. Thus Advaitic method of meditation is more integrative. When every worldly phenomenon is discarded, one has to concentrate the mind on the inmost self and meditate on it as Brahman. In the one case it is complete separation from the Spirit, while in the other it is total fusion with the Self.

We shall sum up this section on the meaning of meditation and hold the view that yogic and non-dualistic meditation are not the same. Yoga as a technique is not necessarily religious, whereas meditation is always associated with religious ideas.

---

68 We substitute Nature for *prakṛti* and Spirit for *puruṣa* throughout the study. The two terms are frequent in the third chapter.

Chapter II

THE WAYS AND FORMS OF MEDITATION

A. Introduction

From an investigation into the meaning of meditation, we have seen it as the key to God-realization. If meditation has such an important place in the experience of God, we should then investigate the methods and means of its practice. In this chapter we shall see the Advaitic practice of meditation, leaving aside, however, the treatment of the technique of meditation to the third chapter of our study.

Unfortunately we do not have an adequate presentation of the subject in Swami Prabhavananda. In his writings on meditation he has left us only some scattered hints regarding the methods of meditation. In his exposition of the philosophy of the Upaniṣads [1] he says that in the Upaniṣads there are only certain hints regarding the methods of meditation and no full details. He justifies this Upaniṣadic tendency for the following reasons: [2]

(1) The Upaniṣads are sacred revelations which the ancients did not want to reduce to writing.

(2) In the Upaniṣadic times, even as today, spiritual instruction was communicated orally and not in written form.

(3) There is no common standard method of meditation. Each aspirant should find out his own method of meditation. A particular method suited to the taste and temperament of one aspirant may be useless for another.

(4) The special nature and exact method of meditation should be learnt from one's own spiritual master whose main duty is to study the psychological aspirations of his disciples and to prescribe for each one the appropriate method of meditation.

---

[1] Cf. Swami Prabhavananda, SHI, pp. 39ff.

[2] Cf. *ibid.*, pp. 66-67.

With the few hints available to us, we shall try, as completely as possible, to construct the structure of meditation and to answer the question:

How to meditate?

B. Forms of God; Forms of the Objects of Meditation

All the major Upaniṣads have discussions on the method of meditation as a practical discipline. The Bṛhad-āraṇyaka Upaniṣad instructs that the Self is to be made the object of meditation.[3] The Chāndogya Upaniṣad, which contains a long discourse on meditation in the instruction of Nārada by Sanatkumāra, speaks of worshipping Meditation as Brahman:

> Meditation (*dhyāna*), assuredly, is more than Thought. The earth meditates, as it were (*iva*). The atmosphere meditates, as it were. The heaven meditates, as it were. Water meditates, as it were. Mountains meditate, as it were. Gods and men meditate, as it were. Therefore whoever among men here attain greatness — they have, as it were, a part of the reward of meditation. Now, those who are small are quarrelers, tale-bearers, slanderers. But those who are superior — they have, as it were, a part of the reward of Meditation. Reverence Meditation (CU 7.6.1).

In the introduction to the Śvetāśvatara Upaniṣad Swami Prabhavananda says that practice of meditation according to accepted rules is demanded.[4] It is the means to realize both the formless Brahman as well as Brahman with form. The Upaniṣad indeed says:

> Those who followed after meditation (*dhyāna*) and abstraction (*yoga*)
> Saw the self-power (*ātma-śakti*) of God (*deva*) hidden in his own qualities (*guṇa*)
>
> (SU 1.3).

The Taittirīya Upaniṣad, the greatest preoccupation of which is the knowledge of Brahman,[5] going a step further, teaches that a seeker has as his choice various aspects of God to meditate upon, and

[3] Cf. BU 2.4.5; 4.5.6.

[4] Cf. Swami Prabhavananda, tr., *The Upanishads,* Introduction to the Śvetāśvatara Upaniṣad, p. 117.

[5] The 3 chapters of the Taittirīya Upaniṣad form the 3 'vallis' of the Upaniṣad. They are (1) Śikṣā valli (2) Brahmānanda valli and (3) Bhṛgu valli. Of these the last two vallis deal with knowledge of Brahman.

he becomes eventually identified with the particular form that he chooses:

> ... One should worship It as greatness; one becomes great.
> One should worship It as mind (*manas*); one becomes possessed of mindfulness.
> One should worship It as adoration; desires make adoration to one.
> One should worship It as magic formula (*brahma*); one becomes possessed of magic formula.
> One should worship It as 'the dying around the magic formula' (*brahmaṇaḥ parimara*); around one die his hateful rivals, and those who are his unfriendly foes
>
> (TU 3.10.3-4).

Such meditation is the way to attain unity with Brahman. It shakes off the individual differences and enables us to know Brahman. Meditating on Śiva, the sage reaches the source of all beings.[6]

Thus we come to the conclusion that forms of meditation correspond to the forms of God. In other words, there are as many forms of the object of meditation as there are forms of God. Infinite is God who can assume to Himself infinite forms. However, basing ourselves on the Upaniṣads,

> There are, assuredly, two forms of Brahma: the formed (*mūrta*) and the formless, the mortal and the immortal, the stationary and the moving, the actual (*sat*) and the yon (*tya*)
>
> (BU 2. 3. 1)
>
> There are, assuredly, two forms of Brahma: the formed and the formless. Now, that which is the formed is unreal; that which is the formless is real, is Brahma, is light
>
> (Maitrī U 6.3),

we accept the following fundamental division:

1. God with form
2. God without form

1. *God with Form*

The Absolute of the Upaniṣads, called Brahman, is described under two aspects: Brahman without quality (Nirguṇa Brahman) and Brahman with quality (Saguṇa Brahman).[7] The former is the form-

---

[6] Cf. Kaivalya U 5-10.

[7] Other terms for Nirguṇa Brahman and Saguṇa Brahman respectively are: Higher Brahman (Parā Brahman) and Lower Brahman (Aparā Brahman), Quality-less Brahman

less Absolute. Any resemblance to anything human is denied It, to the extent that It is not even referred to by 'he' or 'him.' It is neuter and is referred to as That or It. Brahman with quality is referred to by the masculine He. He is known as Īśvara. Īśvara is Brahman conditioned by the creative power called *māyā.* But quality-less Brahman and Brahman with quality are not two distinct realities, two Brahmans as it were, but two aspects of one and the same reality. Swami Prabhavananda puts the question:

> Are there then two Gods — one the impersonal Brahman, the other the personal Īśwara? No — for Brahman appers as Īśwara only when viewd in the relative ignorance of māyā.[8]

They are not two kinds of Brahman, but only two angles of vision of the same reality of Brahman. According to Advaita they are like the sea and its waves.[9]

Brahman with quality is the cause of the universe and its animating principle. To Him all perfections are attributed. He is all-knowing, all-powerful and the supreme Lord.[10] Known as Brahmā, Viṣṇu and Śiva, He is the principle behind creation, preservation and destruction of the universe. As the inner controller (*antaryāmin*), He guides the activities of all creatures. It is He who gives reality to all modifications in the universe. The different incarnations (*avatāra*) are His manifestations. He is an important factor in man's spiritual development. A beginner in spiritual life finds it hard to meditate on the formless Absolute. For his benefit, therefore, the Upaniṣads describe Brahman with form as a support for meditation.

But according to Swami Prabhavananda the conditioning of Brahman is only apparent. Brahman, which has no form, undergoes the limitations only to explain the universe. Swami Prabhavananda says:

> Brahman, being the Absolute, is beyond all action. Therefore, Brahman cannot be said to create or to destroy. It is Ishwara, Brahman united to His power who creates this universe, preserves it and dissolves it.[11]

(Nirviśeṣa Brahman) and Brahman with quality (Saviśeṣa Brahman), Unconditioned Brahman (Nirvikalpa Brahman) and Conditioned Brahman (Savikalpa Brahman).

8 Swami Prabhavananda, SHI, p. 289.

9 Other schools of Vedānta do not admit this distinction. Rāmānuja, the exponent of qualified non-dualism, rejects the distinction between Brahman with attributes and Brahman without them.

10 Omniscient, cf. MU 1.1.9; Omnipotent, cf. SU 6.8; Supreme Lord, cf. BU 3.8.9.

11 Swami Prabhavananda, *Song of God,* pp. 272-273.

Īśvara is Brahman Itself, which puts on a name and a form (*nāma rūpa*) and appears to be so only as long as the phenomenal universe of name and form appears to be real. In the ultimate analysis what persists is Brahman alone. This accounts for the spiritual significance of the concept of Īśvara. As Swami Prabhavananda says: "The conception of Ishwara represents all that the human intellect can know of God." [12]

2. *God without Form*

The Indo-Aryan thinkers, after long consideration, came to the conclusion that behind the universe there is a primary reality. The word used in the Upaniṣads to indicate the supreme Reality is Brahman. Brahman, the key concept of the Vedic religion, is the reality experienced as the first principle. According to Swami Prabhavananda, Brahman is the single, central fact of Vedic cosmology. It is one of the two pillars — the other being Ātman — on which rests the whole edifice of Indian philosophy.[13] It is said:

> Filled with Brahman are the things we see;
> Filled with Brahman are the things we see not;
> From out of Brahman floweth all that is;
> From Brahman all — yet is he still the same.[14]

From It come all things, by It are they sustained and into It do they return.

Some Upaniṣads teach that the formless Brahman is real, whereas Brahman with form is unreal.[15] The formed Brahman is the effect and the formless is the cause. In deep meditation one experiences Brahman as the formless Absolute. It is at a lower state of consciousness that Brahman with form is experienced. According to Advaita one worships Brahman with form in the ordinary state of consciousness; in the experience of the formless Absolute one loses the sense of individuality.

The word Brahman is derived from the root *bṛh* meaning 'to grow,' 'to burst forth.' [16] The derivation *brahman* seems to have

[12] *Ibid.*, p. 273.
[13] Cf. SWAMI PRABHAVANANDA, *Vedic Religion and Philosophy*, p. 45.
[14] Peace chant in the Upaniṣads of the White Yajur Veda. Translated by Swami Prabhavananda in: SHI, p. 43.
[15] Cf. Maitrī U 6.3.
[16] R. C. Zaehner examines the term *bṛhat* which is adjective, meaning great or large and concludes that one cannot be conclusive about it. Because the word

meant in the beginning 'sacred knowledge,' 'incantation of a hymn' or 'prayer.' Gradually it acquired the meaning of power or potency of prayer, possibly during the struggle for Kṣatriya supremacy. It has a mysterious power and contains within itself the essence of the things denoted. In the Brāhmaṇas *brahman* stood for the ritual and was considered omnipotent. He who knows *brahman* knows and controls the universe (Śatapata Brāhmaṇa x.3.5.11). In later thought, *brahman* meant sacred wisdom, the creative principle and the world-ground — a power that created, pervaded and upheld the totality of existence. That Brahman actually is everything is stated in the Muṇḍaka Upaniṣad:

Brahma, indeed, is this immortal. Brahma before,
Brahma behind, to right and to left.
Stretched forth below and above,
Brahma, indeed, is this whole world, this widest extent
(MU 2.2.11).

One of the representatives of the early Upaniṣadic thinking, the Bṛhad-āraṇyaka Upaniṣad, records some most important passages on Brahman. In BU 3.9.1-9 Yājñavalkya reduces the popular number of 3306 gods to one, and that one was Brahman, called 'that' (*tyad*). Another passage which shows the importance of the doctrine of Brahman is BU 3.6. Gārgī, one of the two women philosophers in the Upaniṣads, insisted on the ultimate world-ground. When she finally came up to Brahman, Yājñavalkya warned: 'Gārgī, do not question too much, lest your head fall off. In truth, you are questioning too much about a divinity about which further questions cannot be asked. Gārgī, do not over-question' (BU 3.6). In another most important passage, which arrives at a progressive definition of

---

originally meant sacred word or sacred formula. Cf. R. C. Zaehner, *Hinduism* (London, 1962), pp. 60ff. Max Müller comes to the conclusion that the etymological meaning of Brahman is doubtful, but he affirms that It originally meant "what bursts forth or breaks forth, whether in shape of thought and word, or in the shape of creative power or physical force." Max Müller, *Three Lectures on the Vedānta Philosophy* (Varanasi, 1967), p. 22. Paul Deussen takes the root *brah* which literally means swelling, but applied to prayer as the "will of man striving toward the holy, the divine." Paul Deussen, *The System of the Vedānta* (Delhi, 1972), p. 120. But A. B. Keith holds that there is no actual support of the Ṛg Veda for the view both of Max Müller and Paul Deussen. Cf. A. B. Keith, *The Religion and Philosophy of the Veda and Upanishads* 2 vols. (Cambridge-Massachusetts, 1925), vol. 1, p. 445. In the Ṛg Veda the word *brahman* means sacred knowledge, but it underwent many developments. Therefore in studying the etymological meaning of the word *brahman* one should not forget the process of evolution it underwent.

Brahman, King Ajātaśatru concludes that Brahman is the truth of truths, the Ultimate Truth:

> As a spider might come out with his thread, as small sparks come forth from the fire, even so from this Soul come forth all vital energies (*prāṇa*), all worlds, all gods, all beings. The mystic meaning (*upaniṣad*) thereof is 'the Real of the real' (*satyasya satya*). Vital energies, verily, are the real. He is their Real'
>
> (BU 2.1.20).

In order to show that Brahman is not merely a featureless Absolute, but is all this universe, Swami Prabhavananda translates SU 4.2-4, varying slightly from the original:

> O Brahman Supreme!
> Thou art the fire,
> Thou art the sun,
> Thou art the air,
> Thou art the moon,
> Thou art the starry firmament,
> Thou art Brahman Supreme:
> Thou art the waters — thou,
> The creator of all!
> Thou art woman, thou art man,
> Thou art the youth, thou art the maiden,
> Thou art the old man tottering with his staff;
> Thou facest everywhere.
> Thou art the dark butterfly,
> Thou art the green parrot with red eyes,
> Thou art the thunder cloud, the seasons, the seas.
> Without beginning art thou,
> Beyond time, beyond space.
> Thou art he from whom sprang
> The three worlds.[17]

Brahman is both transcendent and immanent. To explain this latter aspect he quotes the Muṇḍaka Upaniṣad 2.2.1-2:

> Self-luminous is Brahman, ever present in the hearts of all. He is the refuge of all, he is the supreme goal. In him exists all that moves and breathes. In him exists all that is. He is both that which is gross and that which is subtle. Adorable is he. Beyond the ken of the senses is he. Supreme is he. Attain thou him!

---

[17] SWAMI PRABHAVANANDA, tr., *The Upanishads,* pp. 123-124. He quotes this passage in order to refute the alleged pantheism in Indian thought. Admitted that the universe emanated from Brahman, he says that despite this emanation 'yet is he still the same' (reference to Peace Chant in the Upaniṣads of the White Yajur Veda) and concludes that there cannot be pantheism in this sense.

> He the self-luminous, subtler than the subtlest, in whom exist all the worlds and all those that live therein — he is the imperishable Brahman. He is the principle of life. He is speech, and he is mind. He is real. He is immortal. Attain him, O my friend, the one goal to be attained! [18]

Brahman, strictly taken, is without difference (*nirviśeṣa*), without qualities (*nirguṇa*), without limitations (*nirupādhika*), and without form (*nirākara*). Therefore It cannot be described in words. Brahman is describable only negatively (BU 2.3.6). Any description makes It something. But It is nothing among things. It is beyond time, space and cause.[19] The mind cannot reach It, for It is not related to anything; the intellect cannot perceive It, for It is incomprehensible, uninferable and unthinkable. The best way to speak of It is to remain silent.[20]

The Upaniṣad repeatedly teaches that our knowledge of Brahman is *neti, neti!* it is not thus, it is not thus.[21] Human thought and words are inaccessible in front of It. The sages sometimes felt that no affirmation whatever regarding Brahman could be made. It escapes all definition, all description. As the Taittirīya Upaniṣad teaches, words turn back from Brahman, and mind comes away baffled, unable to reach It (TU 2.4). Therefore the only way of speaking about Brahman is the denial of all the terms of ordinary knowledge. All that could be said of It is an everlasting 'No'. It is the negative of every affirmation. Its existence is on a transcendental level. Śaṁkara calls It non-dual (*a-dvaitam*). It is one and admits not a second (CU 6.2.1; Kaivalya U 19). We do not know Its nature since It is the 'wholly other.' For It is soundless, touchless, formless,

---

[18] *Ibid.*, pp. 45-46.

[19] Brahman is beyond time: cf. BU 4.4.16; KU 6.1; SU 5.13.
Brahman is beyond space: cf. BU 3.8.8; KU 2.20; CU 3.14.3.
Brahman is beyond cause: cf. BU 4.4.20.

[20] Śaṁkara in his commentary on the *Vedānta Sūtras* III.ii.1 relates how the sage Bāhva, being questioned about Brahman by Vāṣkalin, explained it to him by silence. He said to Vāṣkalin: "Learn Brahman, O friend," and became silent. Then, on a second and third questioning, Bāhva replied: "I am teaching you indeed, but you do not understand. Silent is that Self." Swami Prabhavananda says that this passage from an Upaniṣad no longer extant is preserved only in Śaṁkara's commentary. Cf. Swami Prabhavananda, SHI, p. 45.

[21] Cf. BU 2.3.6; 4.2.4; 4.4.22; 4.5.15 "idam na, idam na." "Another method of approach," says Swami Prabhavananda, "more acceptable perhaps to our human minds, is to say: "Brahman is not this, Brahman is not that ...," until the entire phenomenal universe has been eliminated, and Brahman alone remains." Swami Prabhavananda, *Song of God*, pp. 271-272.

tasteless, odorless, without beginning, without end and higher than the great (KU 3.15).

The only assertion that we can make of formless Brahman is that It is not this or that. Examining every object in the phenomenal universe, one finds that Brahman is not this. It is other than what we know (Kena U 3). The Gītā says that It is neither the Existent nor the non-Existent (BG 13.12). It is non-Being in the sense that It is not the being which is usually meant. It is a Being beyond all other beings. One can at best say what Brahman is not, not what It is.

The sage Yājñavalkya calls Brahman the Imperishable (*akṣaram*) (BU 3.8.8). It is neither a substance nor a possessor of attributes. What counts most, according to him, is the knowledge of this Imperishable (BU 3.8.10). This Brahman, which is beyond mind and speech, and defined as *neti, neti,* is unseen but is the Seer; unheard but is the Hearer; unthought but is the Thinker, unknown but is the Knower (BU 3.8.11).

Although *neti, neti* is negative in form its content is highly positive. Brahman is not non-entity. It is the 'reality of reality.'[22] The Upaniṣads define Brahman as 'the real, as the knowledge and as the infinite,'[23] as the bliss[24] and as knowledge and bliss.[25] Advaita often describes It as *Satcidānanda,*[26] a compound term consisting of three words: *Sat* (Existence), *Cit* (Consciousness) and *Ānanda* (Bliss). Brahman is Existence. It is, and It alone is, the true existence, ever the same in past, present and future. Brahman does not exist like any other object, but as absolute existence. In the same way, Consciousness and Bliss enter into Its very nature. Pure Being is at once Pure Consciousness and Pure Bliss. This is because It is absolute Being, absolute Consciousness and absolute Bliss.[27]

Brahman, though incomprehensible (*agṛhyaḥ*), is not unknow-

---

22 *'satyasya satyam,'* BU 2.3.6.

23 *"satyaṁ jñānam anantham,"* TU 2.1.

24 *"ānando brahmeti vyajānāt,"* TU 3.6.

25 *"vijñānam ānandam brahma,"* BU 3.9.28.

26 This description of Brahman is not found as such in any of the principal Upaniṣads or in Śaṁkara. It first occurs in the Nṛsiṅha-tāpanīya-Upaniṣad (*Ind. St.* IX, 60.84.143.147.148.154).

27 These are not Its attributes, but Its very nature. Swami Prabhavananda explains: "The Upanishads say that Brahman is Existence, Knowledge and Bliss; but these are not attributes. Brahman is Existence itself. Brahman is not wise or happy, but absolute Knowledge, absolute Joy." SWAMI PRABHAVANANDA, *Song of God,* p. 271.

able. The truth of Brahman is revealed to the seeker who sinks himself in pious meditation (*pra-ṇi-dhānam*). In the following two sections we shall see how we can meditate on God under both His aspects — with form and without form.

C. Meditation on God with form

The path to formless Brahman is steep and adventurous. Only the specially qualified aspirants can directly meditate on It. Therefore, the sacred texts recommend others to meditate on Brahman with form. In this section we shall discuss the following forms of meditation: repetition of the name of God, *upāsanā*, meditation on the mystical symbol OM and the loving meditation.

1. *Repetition of the Name of God*

In the path to meditation the seeker will eventually meet with many obstacles. The Hindu mystics, having foreseen these dangers in meditation, have developed a science called *mantra-vidyā*, a technique of repeating the name of God. Repetition of the name of God, they say, protects the soul. What Śrī Chaitanya, the sixteenth century Bengal mystic, says in a prayer indicates the Hindu mentality:

> Chant the Name of the Lord and His Glory unceasingly
> That the mirror of the heart may be wiped clean
> And quenched that mighty forest fire,
> Worldly lust, raging furiously within.[28]

At the very outset two Sanskrit terms have to be explained. The one is *mantra.* Literally it means that which when reflected upon gives liberation.[29] Down from the Vedic age it has been held in high esteem. Tracing the history of Hindu *mantra,* M. Dhavamony says:

> From the ancient times, the *mantra* form of worship, owing its origin to the conception of the mystery of speech as that which expresses thought, has played an important part in the life and worship of the Hindus.[30]

---

[28] Śrī Chaitanya, "Chant the Name of the Lord," trans. from the original Sanskrit by Swami Prabhavananda and Christopher Isherwood, in: *Vedanta for the Western World,* p. 225.

[29] Cf. J. Gonda, *Les Religions de l'Inde* (Payot, Paris, 1962-1966), tome 1ʳ, p. 34 n. 1.

[30] M. Dhavamony, "Hindu Prayer," in: *Studia Missionalia,* 24 (1975) 195.

The Vedic poets understood it as a solemn formula, possessing some divine power, when uttered in a definite rhythm. But more simply, it is an embodiment in sound of a particular god or goddess or the Supreme Being itself.

The *guru* initiates the aspirant by giving him a divine name of his own. Swami Prabhavananda asks him not to reveal it to any other human being.[31] He has to use it for prayer and meditation as a means to enter into communion with the deity.

The other term is *japa.* Its root meaning is muttering or whispering. It is the methodical repetition of the divine name in a whispering tone. It is likened to a chain, holding which one reaches the thing to which it is tied. Each *japa* brings the meditant nearer to his goal, God.[32] Even more significant is the psychology behind the repetition of God's name. This act brings God's presence. Hindus believe that repetition of the name of God, while meditating on it, has the power to inspire the worshipper's thought. As a result of repeating God's name the meditator increases his introspective power; his mental and physical obstacles disappear; slowly the mind inclines toward meditation.

2. *Upāsanā*

Upāsanā, or meditative worship, is directed to Brahman with form. The sages recognized its special spiritual power and prescribed it to the whole Hindu society. Different meditations were sought out to fit the different states of the people. They believed that mere mechanical performance of the sacrifice brought them no spiritual benefit. To render it spiritually fruitful they began to introduce meditation on it. The opening verse of the Maitrī Upaniṣad is a clear indication of this:

> That which for the ancients was [merely] a building up [of sacrificial fires] was, verily, a sacrifice to Brahma. Therefore with the building of these sacrificial fires the sacrificer should meditate upon the Soul (Ātman). So, verily, indeed, does the sacrifice become really complete and indeficient (Maitrī U 1.1).

In order that the sacrifice may become perfect, the sacrificer was asked to meditate. By this act the ceremonial ritual is converted into a spiritual travail. The acts accompanied by meditative insight

[31] Cf. Swami Prabhavananda on *Yoga-sūtra* I.29.

[32] Cf. *Gospel,* p. 552.

(*upaniṣadā yogena*) effect a spiritual transformation (CU 1.1.10). Meditative worship on the syllable of the *Udgīta* — the hymn to be sung by the priests of the Sāma Veda — is the subject of a whole section of the Bṛhad-āraṇyaka Upaniṣad (BU 1.3).

The Upaniṣads abound in examples of *upāsanā*. Two sections of the Chāndogya Upaniṣad (CU 3.16-17) are a symbolic meditation on human life as a sacrifice. This meditation is "the richest storehouse of Upaniṣadic meditation." [33] Having divided the human life into three stages, the Upaniṣad compares it to the three parts of a sacrifice. Accordingly, the first twenty-four years of a person are the morning libation (*prātaḥ-savanaṁ*), performed under the Vasus; his next forty-four years are the second part of the sacrifice called the midday libation (*mādhyan-dinaṁ-savanaṁ*), presided over by the Rudras; his last stage of forty-eight years are the third libation (*tṛtīya-savanaṁ*). Thus the whole life of a person is a sacrifice.

Another example of *upāsanā* in the Upaniṣads is the doctrine of the Five Fires (*pañcāgni-vidyā*), which King Pravāhaṇa Jaivali taught Śvetaketu, the son of Aruṇi (BU 6.2.9-13; CU 5.4-8). The doctrine is the answer to the five questions of the King (BU 6.2.2; CU 5.3. 2-3). At death people pass through five sacrificial fires which purify them. The other world, the god of rain (Parjanya), the earth, man and woman are the five sacrificial fires. Those who meditate, knowing the secret of these fires, are rewarded.

In the *Śāṇḍilya vidyā* (CU 3.14.1-4) one is asked to meditate tranquilly on the whole world as Brahman (*sarvam khalv idam brahma*). The eternal principle of all beings lives, whole and undivided, in the heart of man. Even more, it spreads its presence everywhere (SU 4.3-4). Through the simile of the 'city of Brahman' the *Dahara vidyā* (*daharam* = small) provides a meditation, according to which he (the self) is in the heart.[34]

These are but a few examples of the Upaniṣadic meditations. With these examples in mind we shall try to see the theological and spiritual contents of *upāsanā*.

Upāsanā, which is worship, especially worship associated with meditation on a deity, literally means, like the word Upaniṣad, sitting near, mentally approaching an ideal. The element of devotion is a special characteristic of *upāsanā*. It is not possible to worship the

---

[33] SWAMI GAMBHIRANANDA, "Upaniṣadic meditation," in: *The Cultural Heritage of India* vol. I (Calcutta, reprint 1970), p. 376.

[34] Cf. CU 8.1.1 *hṛidi* + *ayam* = *hṛidayam* = he is in the heart.

formless Absolute, but one can worship God. *Upāsanā* is devout meditation. It is not mere thought. It employs some kind of symbol to support the mind. For it is easier to hold the mind on a concrete object rather than on an abstract idea. Thus the Muṇḍaka Upaniṣad 2.1.4 gives an *upāsanā* furnished with a number of symbols. The divine and formless person meditated upon is said to have fire as his head, the sun and the moon as his eyes, space as his ears, the Vedas as his voice and the world as his head. In the Chāndogya Upaniṣad 1.8-9 there is an outstanding example of a meditation which leads up to the Absolute.

The similes employed in the Upaniṣads indicate that *upāsanā* is predominently an act of volition rather than that of intellect. In the analogy of a man and wife in embrace (BU 4.3.21), the aspects of love and divine communion are symbolized. The Taittirīya Upaniṣad teaches that meditation on Brahman as seated in the heart is helpful (TU 1.6.1). He who meditates in the manner prescribed by the scriptures even becomes Brahman (TU 1.6.2). Stating the principles of self-contemplation (*adhyātma-yoga*), the Kaṭha Upaniṣad teaches that immediate relationship with God is the fruit of continued meditation (KU 2.12).

The principle behind *upāsanā* is that man is not only an intellectual being, but also has emotions. It is not advisable to destroy the emotions; but to give them an orientation to God is the right thing. *Upāsanā* does this by deepening the meditator's emotions, elevating his feelings and strengthening his will. This shows an advanced stage of spiritual growth.

Having examined the meaning and spiritual significance of *upāsanā*, we shall now see an important type of meditation with the help of a sound symbol of Brahman.

3. *The Mystical Symbol OM*

The sacred syllable OM, sometimes spelled A U M, infinitely prolonged, is perhaps the most significant of all symbols of meditation. Swami Prabhavananda considers it an aid to realize God. He says that from Vedic times until the present day this one-syllabic prayer has been taken as an aid to meditation by all spiritual aspirants.[35]

OM is the representative in sound of the total Brahman, both

---

[35] Cf. SWAMI PRABHAVANANDA, "The Mystic Word "OM", in: *Vedanta for the Western World,* p. 149.

the higher and the lower. The word first appears in the Taittirīya Saṁhitā of the Black Yajur Veda III.2.9.6. It is like the 'Amen' responded by the *adhvaryu* priest to each Ṛg Vedic verse uttered by the *Hotṛ*. Slowly there evolved the custom of beginning every Vedic chant with the syllable OM (CU 1.4.1,4).

The importance attached to this sacred syllable in Hinduism is clear from the following stanzas of the Gītā:

> OM TAT SAT. This is declared to be the threefold designation of Brahman. By this were Brāhmaṇas, Vedas, and sacrifices ordained of old.
> Therefore with utterance of OM are the rites of sacrifice, almsgiving, and austerity, enjoined by ordinance, ever begun by those who study Brahman (BG 17.23-24).

This word expressed Brahman. Therefore a man who begins and ends every ritual utterance with this sacred syllable attains to Brahman.

With the identification of OM with Brahman, the Upaniṣadic reflection on OM reaches a turning point. The Taittirīya Upaniṣad 1.8.1 says that OM is Brahman (*aum iti brahma*). The same is said also in the Kaṭha Upaniṣad:

> The word which all the Vedas rehearse,
> And which all austerities proclaim,
> Desiring which men live the life of religious studentship (*brahmacarya*) —
> That word to thee I briefly declare.
> That is *Om!*
> That syllable, truly, indeed, is Brahma!
> That syllable indeed is the supreme!
> Knowing that syllable, truly, indeed,
> Whatever one desires is his! (KU 2.15-16)

Sage Pippalāda taught that OM is the higher and the lower Brahman (Praśna U 5.2).[36] Concerning the mystic symbolism of the word OM, the Māṇḍūkya Upaniṣad says:

> *Om!* — This syllable is this whole world.
> Its further explanation is: —
> The past, the present, the future — everything is just the word *Om*.
> And whatever else that transcends threefold time — that, too, is just the word *Om* (Mā U 1).

---

36 OM is also known as *oṁkāra, praṇava* and *ekākṣaram*.

Being the most adequate symbol of Brahman, OM is a means of meditation on Brahman. This is the central theme of the Māṇḍūkya Upaniṣad which is said to be an exposition of the principle of OM. Being "the great weapon of the Upaniṣads" (MU 2.2.3), it is the foremost symbol in the Upaniṣadic meditation. A very extensive teaching on OM is also given in the Maitrī Upaniṣad 6. There OM is an instrument in the technique of meditation. It produces consciousness (*caitanya*) in the mind. In this sense OM is called a sacred seed-word (*vīja-mantra*).

On the several Upaniṣadic meditations on OM the one in the Muṇḍaka Upaniṣad deserves special attention:

> Taking as a bow the great weapon of the Upaniṣad,
> One should put upon it an arrow sharpened by meditation.
> Stretching it with a thought directed to the essence of That,
> Penetrate that Imperishable as the mark, my friend.
> The mystic syllable *Om* (*praṇava*) is the bow. The arrow is the soul (*ātman*).
> Brahman is said to be the mark (*lakṣya*).
> By the undistracted man is It to be penetrated.
> One should come to be in It, as the arrow [in the mark]
> (MU 2.2.3-4).

The same meditation is given in the Maitrī Upaniṣad 6.24 although there are some slight verbal variations. A sublime meditation on OM is also to be found in the Śvetāśvatara Upaniṣad:

> As the material form (*mūrti*) of fire when latent in its source [i. e. the fire-wood]
> Is not perceived — and yet there is no evanishment of its subtle form (*liṅga*) —
> But may be caught again by means of the drill in its source,
> So, verily, both [the universal and the individual Brahma]
> are to be found in the body by the use of *Om*.
> By making one's own body the lower friction-stick
> And the syllable *Om* the upper friction-stick,
> By practising the friction of meditation (*dhyāna*),
> One may see the God (*deva*) who is hidden, as it were
> (SU 1.13-14).

Here the sage speaks of two firesticks: one is the body and the other is the syllable OM.[37] By rubbing the two, the fire of knowledge is kindled. The hidden fire becomes manifest through the friction.

---

37 Cf. also Kaivalya U 11.

In the same way, by practising meditation with the help of OM one may get the vision of God.

Concerning the mystic syllable's power of leading to Brahma-realization, there is the following account in the Praśna Upaniṣad. Swami Prabhavananda translates Question 5.1-5 as follows:

> Whereupon Satyakama, coming near to the master, said:
> "Venerable sir, if a man meditate upon the syllable OM all his life, what shall be his reward after death?"
> And the master answered him thus:
> "Satyakama, OM is Brahman — both the conditioned and the unconditioned, the personal and the impersonal. By meditating upon it the wise man may attain either the one or the other.
> "If he meditate upon OM with but little knowledge of its meaning, but nevertheless is enlightened thereby, upon his death he will be immediately born again on this earth, and during his new life he will be devoted to austerity, continence, and faith, and will attain to spiritual greatness.
> "If, again, he meditate upon OM with a greater knowledge of its meaning, upon his death he will ascend to the lunar heaven, and after he has partaken of its pleasures will return again to earth.
> "But if he meditate upon OM in the full consciousness that it is one with God, upon his death he will be united with the light that is in the sun, he will be freed from evil, even as a snake is freed from its slough, and he will ascend to God's dwelling place. There he will realize Brahman, who evermore abides in the heart of all beings — Brahman Supreme! [38]

In the above Upaniṣadic meditation we see that OM has the function of supplying the mind with a symbol to fix on. With its help, the meditant succeeds in concentrating his imagination and reflection. By constant practice he no longer needs a symbol; the symbol is then substituted by vision. At this stage his meditation grows in intensity and becomes what is called 'loving meditation.'

4. *Loving Meditation*

Meditation, as seen in the light of *Bhakti-mārga,* is an expression of supreme love. Meditation, which is an uninterrupted thought flowing toward God, becomes easier for a lover of God.

With this in mind the Hindu mystics have developed the doctrine of the Chosen Ideal (*Iṣṭa*). "The deity, in whose *mantra* a Hindu is initiated, and to whom he looks for special aid in the attainment

---

[38] SWAMI PRABHAVANANDA, tr., *The Upanishads,* p. 40.

of salvation, is called the chosen deity." [39] There are only those very rare people, specially gifted, who can concentrate on the formless Absolute. In every age they are outnumbered by those who take an aspect of God as the object of meditation.

Swami Prabhavananda puts forward a fundamental reason for the development of the concept of the chosen deity in Hindu spirituality. He writes:

> The spirit of catholicity is a prominent feature of all Indian teachings. They evince a spirit of harmony rather than of conflict, of synthesis and toleration rather than of opposition and sectarianism. Infinite is God, infinite are his aspects, and infinite are the ways to reach him. In the Atharva Veda we read: Ekaṁ jyotir bahudhā bibhāti — The one Light appears in diverse forms. This ideal of harmony has held its own in India down to the present time.[40]

God, who is infinite, has infinite expressions. The absolute Existence-Knowledge-Bliss is inexpressible and infinite, that It manifests Itself in infinite ways. Śrī Rāmakṛṣṇa's illustration of water in the lake may be taken. The water, which is formless, assumes the forms of the vessels in which it is filled. So also the one God assumes many forms for the sake of humanity. Different religions worship God in His different manifestations. The different deities are different doors, as it were, to the one God.

There is absolute freedom in choosing the deity. But once the choice is made, it remains definite and final. To change one's chosen deity day by day blocks spiritual progress. Swami Prabhavananda seems to be uncompromising on this point when he says that the tender plant of spirituality will die if exposed too early to a constant change of chosen ideals to meditate on.[41]

After having chosen the form of God, the spiritual aspirant is asked to concentrate and meditate on it. He consecrates himself to the chosen deity. It should be the destination of all his thoughts.

By directing the mind to the chosen deity, the meditator establishes an emotional bond with it. It is natural to think of beloved people. A mother thinks of her child and a husband his wife. So also when there is an emotional bond between the meditator and the chosen deity, the former is lost in the divine bliss. For he participates

---

[39] M. DHAVAMONY, "Hindu Prayer," in: *Studia Missionalia,* 24 (1975) 195.
[40] SWAMI PRABHAVANANDA, SHI, p. 97.
[41] Cf. ID., RP, p. 165.

in the bliss of Brahman as graphically described in the Upaniṣad (TU 2.8).

Loving meditation, which is one of the stages of divine inebriation, is a sublimation of the emotional life of man. The Hindu psychology of devotion classifies five types of loving relationship with God. They are commented upon by Swami Prabhavananda.[42] The first is peaceful (*śānta*), the beginning stage of divine love. The second is servitude (*dāsya*), in which God is the Lord and Master whom the devotee serves with the greatest reverence. The attitudes of the servant towards his master, the protected towards the protector are of this type. The third is friendship (*sākhya*). In this the devotee feels that he is a friend and playmate of God. There is a sense of equality between two friends. No barrier of secrets separates them. Next comes tender fondness (*vātsalya*). This is the love of parents towards their children. The devotee takes God for his own child. And lastly comes sweet relation (*mādhurya*), the highest expression of loving relationship. It is the sweet attitude of the lover towards his beloved.

The effects of these various relationships are also described by Swami Prabhavananda. In the first stage the lover of God renounces all attractions of the world. Selfishness gives way to thought of God; self-centredness is replaced by God-centredness. At the second stage, the devotee keeps a respectful distance from his Master, God. The feelings of loyalty and obedience expressed in a total surrender to God are characteristic of this stage. In order to explain the nature of the friendly relationship between man and God, the third stage, Swami Prabhavananda describes Kṛṣṇa as the lover of the shepherdesses. Feelings of intimacy and equality predominate this type of relationship. This signifies a profound change in the feelings and attitudes of the devotee. In the fourth type a deeper attachment to God is felt. Devotion to God is imagined to be nursing one's own child. But the intimacy of loving devotion is felt most in the final stage. The devotee feels it unbearable to be separated from God. He is indeed mad with love. Where is God, the beloved? Sorrow, despair, eagerness and anxiety follow one after another in the search of the heart's delight. The love between Rādhā and Kṛṣṇa is the example par excellence. Such love shows by analogy the most intimate union with God.

---

[42] Cf. Swami Prabhavananda, *Narada's Way of Divine Love*, pp. 139-145.

These are the main types of divine love described in the devotion literature of Hinduism. From the very beginning of his spiritual life the aspirant feels any or several of these types of divine relationship. Now as meditation centres around the chosen deity, the aspirant has to watch over its proceeding and test which type of loving relationship with God is best adapted to him. When he becomes finally certain about it, he can easily foster that relationship during meditation.

The depth of loving meditation corresponds to the intensity of the meditator's love towards the deity. Thought of the deity should permeate his intellect and will. It is a total adherence of the whole person. This enables him, little by little, to withdraw his mind from all other objects. Gradually the whole spiritual forces in the person are awakened and the mind is absorbed in it. In this process three phases can be distinguished: in the first stage, the devotee visualizes only indistinctly parts of the deity's body. This shows that the outside world is still very real to him. As meditation deepens, the figure of the deity becomes more real, and the physical world dreamlike. This is the second stage. Finally, the physical world completely disappers and the ideal appears as a living person, speaking to and guiding the devotee.

For a better understanding of the manner in which a chosen deity aids meditation, the following meditation on Kṛṣṇa may be taken:

In the battlefield of Kurukṣetra the meditant imagines the chariot of Arjuna. The armed chieftains stand in array; the conch-shell horn has sounded; the war is about to start (BG 1.13). At this moment Arjuna seeks Kṛṣṇa's advice. Unwilling to take the life of his kinsmen, Arjuna expresses his state of mind in the words:

> My soul is vexed by the fault of weak compassion; my mind perplexed knows not where duty lies; I ask thee, then; tell me with no uncertain voice which could be better. I am thy disciple; teach me! I come to thee. For I see not clearly aught that may dispel the grief that withers up my senses, though I should win on earth broad sovereignity unrivalled, and lordship even of Heaven's Lords (BG 2.7-8).

After appealing to Kṛṣṇa to instruct him, suddenly, he makes up his mind: 'I will not fight' (BG 2.9).

Kṛṣṇa is Arjuna's charioteer. He is the great god Viṣṇu incarnate. Saying that he consorts with Nature which is his, he asserts himself to be Supreme Being, thus creating confidence in his bosom friend (BG 4.6). The rest of the Gītā is his answer to Arjuna. He sits face to face with Arjuna. A sweet smile rests on his face. His face is the embodiment of serenity. His eyes resemble an ocean of knowledge. He speaks words of wisdom and enlightenment. With facial expressions he tries to convince Arjuna. Those who, knowing his holy birth, take refuge in him, love him alone, meditate on him alone, are not reborn (BG 4.9). By humbly contemplating and approaching him one wins his love (BG 4.10). What Kṛṣṇa demands is that a man should give up all attachments to works and their fruits. This precept he repeats again and again, so that purified from passions, one can walk in his footsteps and is rewarded by his love (BG 4.11). The following three stanzas are said to sum up the whole teaching of the Gītā:

> Hear again my highest word, deepest mystery of all; exceeding beloved art thou of me; therefore shall I declare what is thy weal.
> With mind on me devoutly worship me, to me do sacrifice, to me do reverence; to me shalt thou come; true is my promise to thee; thou art dear to me.
> Abandoning every duty, come to me alone for refuge; I will release thee from all sins; sorrow not! (BG 18.64-66)

Slowly he dispels all the doubts of his friend (BG 18.73). The meditant now imagines himself to be in the place of Arjuna, hearing the message of the Gītā from Kṛṣṇa himself.

Loving meditation, thus, is an important step in the aspirant's relationship with God. Because of his intense love for the chosen deity, his emotional life leads him almost unconsciously to the spiritual progress described above.

Having discussed all the important aspects of loving meditation, we shall now turn our attention to meditation on God without form.

D. Meditation on God without form

Meditation in Advaita finally leads to meditation on the formless Absolute.

There is a paradoxical statement in Swami Prabhavananda's teaching on meditation on God without form which we quote here:

> Now the question is, how is it possible to worship God, to meditate on Him 'whom words cannot express, and from whom the mind comes

> away baffled, unable to reach?' No, it is not possible to contemplate or worship the absolute Reality.[43]

Does this statement mean that meditation on the formless Absolute is impossible? Since the scriptural reference in the above statement is the Taittirīya Upaniṣad 2.4, a reference to quality-less Brahman, undoubtedly he means meditation on the formless Absolute. Therefore, let us start the discussion, of meditation on the formless Absolute, with the question: Is it possible at all to meditate on the formles Abolute?

Quality-less Brahman, as we have observed earlier,[44] is the negation of all attributes and relations. Therefore, one cannot know It in the way one knows an external object.[45] Since the transcendental Absolute remains outside the realm of ordinary thought, external worship and prayer cannot reach It. No symbol can express It. In this sense Advaitins are right, if they mean only some inferior type of meditation.

But Swami Prabhavananda emphatically asserts that meditation on the formless Absolute is possible:

> Brahman, in the absolute sense, cannot possibly be known by the conscious mind. Brahman can only be experienced in that superconscious state achieved by the saints, which is called samadhi ...[46]

This is a higher meditation which has nothing to do with ordinary mental activity. Rather it is a flow of conviction. In *śravaṇa* the spiritual aspirant has already heard the truth. The sacred scriptures and his own spiritual master have provided him with the knowledge of the truth. His remaining task is to realize the truth. It is for this purpose that he resorts to meditation. The truth he has heard must now become *samyagdarśanam* — the higher knowledge of the quality-less Brahman — resulting in an immediate consciousness.[47]

---

[43] SWAMI PRABHAVANANDA, RP, p. 161. Swami Nikhilananda, himself an Advaitin, in his edition of the Upaniṣads, repeatedly says that quality-less Brahman cannot be the object of meditation. Cf. SWAMI NIKHILANANDA, tr., *The Upanishads* (New York, 1963), pp. 39, 44.

[44] See above, pp. 43-48.

[45] "If God were known in the same way as an object is known or perceived, He would still remain unknown ..." SWAMI PRABHAVANANDA, RP, p. 160.

[46] ID., *Song of God*, p. 273.

[47] Śrī Rāmakṛṣṇa says: "On attaining the Knowledge of Brahman and communing with It in nirvikalpa samadhi, one realizes Brahman, the Infinite without form or shape and beyond mind and words." *Gospel*, p. 153.

In this way his meditation on the transcendental Absolute is nothing but an intensification of the truth he has already received. Hindu mystics would compare it to the intensification of light. Therefore, we see that there is no fundamental difference in the contents of his spiritual life in its initiation and consummation — the same truth heard of in the beginning of spiritual life has become his integral experience during the hours of meditation.

Here Swami Prabhavananda's explanation of a mystic cycle is helpful to understand the Advaitic meditation.[48] The mystic cycle is produced by a meditation in different steps. In the primary step the meditant, by an act of discrimination, denies reality to all things other than Brahman. Brahman is neither 'this' nor 'that.' When he becomes absorbed in meditation, he rises above the plane of physical perception. The universe of finite objects and the universe of ideas are wiped out from his consciousness. Swami Prabhavananda calls this an ineffably exalted state beyond the sense of time, space and causation, the conditions of empirical existence. In the second step he returns from the enlightened consciousness either to the normal consciousness or to one between the normal and transcendental consciousness technically called *bhāvamukta*. Even if he is in the normal state of consciousness he still has the memory of the transcendental vision of the Absolute. If he is in the intermediary state of consciousness he has the transcendental vision present in his consciousness. In both cases he lives and acts under the influence of the ineffable experience he had in the height of his meditation.

The Advaitic meditation, in which the formless aspect of Absolute is meditated upon, is the most difficult of all. A knower (*jñāni*) may make use of some of the forms of meditation. Śrī Rāmakṛṣṇa mentions a few classical symbols of meditation.[49] In one, Brahman is an ocean in which the individual self, like a fish, swims. In another the body is a vessel and the mind is water, upon which is reflected Brahman. In a third Brahman is an infinite ocean and the individual self a pot immersed in it. Both the inside and the outside of the pot is the same water — Brahman. And finally, the individual self is a bird, flying through the infinite sky of Brahman.

These are not, in the strict sense, meditation on the formless Absolute. They are only examples of the material infinity called universal space (*mahākaśa*). There is a higher form of infinity called

[48] Cf. Swami Prabhavananda, SHI, pp. 46-47.
[49] Cf. *Gospel*, pp. 906-907.

mental space (*chittākaśa*). Even this is far too inferior to the true infinity of the Spirit, the spiritual infinity (*chidākaśa*). It is beyond all forms and attributes, the *neti, neti* of the Upaniṣads.[50] Advaitic meditation on the formless Absolute is meditation on this third type of infinity.

With this lofty conception of the Absolute the spiritual aspirant begins his meditation. In his search for the Absolute, he analyses all his experiences. He finds the method of *neti, neti* best suited to his beginning stage. He negates all his experiences one by one, till at last he reaches the Absolute. His meditation is a negation of the non-self and an assertion of the Self. It is, as Yājñavalkya explained, neither gross nor fine, neither short nor long, neither shadow nor darkness, nor any one of the opposites (BU 3.8.8). The sun shines not there, nor the moon and the stars; it is the shining light of the universe (MU 2.2.9-10). Brahman is everywhere: in front is Brahman, behind is Brahman, to the right and to the left. It spreads forth below and above (MU 2.2.11). The Muṇḍaka Upaniṣad records two very beautiful meditations. The one is the coming forth of the many sparks from a blazing fire; into the same source they return at the end (MU 2.1.1).[51] The other is the flowing of the rivers into an ocean into which they merge, casting off all individualities (MU 3.2.8).

But the best of all the Advaitic meditations is the meditation on the great sayings. They are the " concise utterances in which the Upaniṣads sum up their whole teaching." [52] The identity of the Self and Brahman is their most significant declaration. There are four great sayings:

1. *Tat tvam asi* — That thou art (CU 6.8.7).
2. *Aham Brahmāsmi* — I am Brahman (BU 1.4.10).
3. *Prajñānaṁ Brahma* — Consciousness is Brahman (AU 3.1.3).
4. *Ayam ātmā Brahma* — This Self is Brahman (Mā U 2).

Each of these utterances declares that the individual self is the same as Brahman. Each is a statement that Brahman is the sole Reality. According to Swami Prabhavananda the fundamental truth of the

---

50 Cf. BU 2.3.6; 4.2.4; 4.4.22; 4.5.15.
51 Cf. also BU 2.1.20.
52 Swami Prabhavananda, SHI, p. 58.

philosophy of the Upaniṣads — the identity between Brahman and Self — is the content of the great sayings.[53]

Of all the great sayings "That thou art" is said to contain the truth of all truths. In declaring it, the sacred text identifies That with thou — the Supreme Self with the individual self. By meditating on the identity of That and thou, the meditator tries to experience himself as the Absolute. Such meditation destroys all doubts. Like the 'amalaka fruit on the palm of the hand' (Paiṅgala U 3.2), the truth of Brahman becomes plain to the meditator's mind. Just as the sun shines forth with splendour when the clouds disappear, incessant meditation on "That thou art" reveals the ultimate oneness of all beings with the Absolute (CU 6.1.4; MU 1.1.3).

In the meditation on "That thou art" there is no experience of a person, nor of interpersonal relationship as would be the case with loving meditation. There is no duality, no distinction between himself (meditator) and the act of meditating. This is the acme of experience. Human experience cannot go beyond absolute oneness.

In this way, according to Swami Prabhavananda meditation on the formless Absolute is the highest form of meditation. " In its highest form, say the Upaniṣads, it is concentration upon the truth of Aham Brahmāsmi (I am Brahman)." [54] The meditator becomes established in the knowledge of the identity of Self and Brahman. This is not an abstract knowledge but the conscious realization of what Brahman is: the absolute Existence-Knowledge-Bliss.

E. Concluding synthesis

We find no better way of concluding this chapter than summarizing the teaching of Swami Prabhavananda himself:

After assuming the posture of meditation, shut the doors to your senses. The idea is that you have to concentrate upon God

---

[53] Cf. Id., *Vedic Religion and Philosophy,* p. 52. Another representative of Advaita, Swami Satprakashananda, interprets the great saying as follows: "The mahāvākya presents in a nutshell the Vedic view of God, the Vedic view of man, and the Vedic view of man's approach to God. It furnishes the clue to his spiritual life. By knowing the self one knows God, the One Self of all. The way to the Supreme Being is an inner approach. It is the gradual realization of the innate Divinity. In fact, the great Vedic dictum makes the inaccessible accessible, the incomprehensible comprehensible, the unknowable knowable." Swami Satprakashananda, *Methods of Knowledge according to Advaita* (London, 1965), p. 201.

[54] Swami Prabhavananda, SHI, p. 66.

within the temple of the body; you have to learn to worship God within yourself. Enter within the chamber of your own heart and see the effulgent Lord. God is beneath your outer consciousness, shining within the lotus of your heart. *See* Him. Feel His presence, *seem* to *see* Him.

Leave the world with all its distractions at the outer gate. Enter alone into the chamber of your heart. Shut the doors and be alone with God. He is, and you are.

At all times form the habit of thinking of God. As you continue in your practice of habitual thinking of God, your mind will be purified, joy and sweetness will overcome in your heart. Absorption in Him will follow in due course. You will become drunk with the intoxicating love of God, and your heart will be illumined by His knowledge.[55]

---

[55] Cf. Id., RP, pp. 168-169.

Chapter III

THE TECHNIQUES OF MEDITATION

A. Introduction

Sage Patañjali, the father of Indian Yoga philosophy, composed the *Yoga-sūtras* to explain Yoga to his contemporaries. Swami Prabhavananda has translated the text with a commentary of his own. His interpretation is however from the Advaita viewpoint. This chapter examines how the Yoga techniques can be fruitfully made use of in meditation.

B. What Yoga is

We shall understand the significance of Yoga in Indian Spirituality a little better if we have some clear ideas about Patañjali's *Yoga-sūtras,* the historical development of Yoga and the philosophical presuppositions of Yoga.

1. *The Yoga-sūtras*

a) The Author

There is a unanimous opinion among scholars that Patañjali's work was not an original exposition of Yoga, but only a systematic compilation. He collected the different Yoga disciplines and grafted them all on the Sāṁkhya metaphysics.

But there has been a long controversy over the identification of the author of the *Yoga-sūtras.* There have been attempts to identify him with Patañjali, the grammarian. Swami Prabhavananda mentions the controversy saying that it is uncertain whether the grammarian and the author of the *Yoga-sūtras* are one and the same.[1]

S. Dasgupta, who has made valuable contributions to the study

[1] Cf. Swami Prabhavananda on *Yoga-sūtra,* p. vii.

of Patañjali, holds the theory that identifies the author of the *Yoga-sūtras* with the writer of the great commentary on Pāṇini called *Mahābhāṣya.* He puts forward a 'legitimate' hypothesis.[2] From the concluding word *iti* of Book III he holds that the work actually ended. But the same word is repeated also at the end of Book IV. From this he infers that the fourth Book is a later interpolation. He holds that the first three Books were composed by Patañjali, the grammarian. He also notes a difference in style of the last Book and the relative shortness of it.

b) The *Yoga-sūtras* and Their Commentaries

Patañjali's *Yoga-sūtras* are divided into four Books: Book I deals extensively with enstasis (*samādhi*).[3] The 51 rules (*sūtras*) explain the goal of enstasis, its kinds and degrees of approach to it. Book II has 55 rules dealing with the means of attaining enstasis. The eight limbs of Yoga come under this part. Book III, consisting of 56 rules, explains the supernatural powers (*vibhūti*) which come to the yogic mind as a result of Yoga practice. The last Book, disproportionately small (34 rules), speaks of isolation (*kaivalya*) which is complete realization according to Yoga. In all therefore the *Yoga-sūtras* consist of 196 rules.

The simplest meaning of the word *sūtra* is thread. As the thread of a garland holds the many flowers together, the *sūtra* maintains the structure of the exposition. The *Yoga-sūtras* were written at a time when there were no books. All the rules had to be memorized. Therefore they had to be comprised in as few words as possible. Often there is no sentence form. Added to this, the use of technical terms and peculiar style rendered the work difficult to understand.

This necessitated commentaries on the *Yoga-sūtras.* Vyāsa was the first to comment on Patañjali. His work is extant under the

---

[2] Cf. S. DASGUPTA, *Yoga Philosophy in Relation to Other Systems of Indian Thought* (Calcutta, 1930), p. 53.

[3] The Sanskrit word *samādhi* is translated differently into English by different scholars. Swami Prabhavananda uses the word 'absorption.' J. H. Woods translates *samādhi* as concentration, *dhyāna* as contemplation and *dhāraṇa* as fixed attention. We avoid Woods' translation as there is risk of confusion between *dhāraṇa* and *samādhi.* S. Dasgupta translates it as 'transe contemplation.' In his *A History of Indian Philosophy* vol. I, p. 272, n. 1 he says that the word *samādhi* cannot properly be translated either by 'concentration' or by 'meditation.' It is the peculiar kind of concentration in the Yoga sense by which the mind becomes one with its object. But a more accurate translation of the Sanskrit word seems to be 'enstasis' and for that reason we shall use that word throughout this study.

title of *Yoga-bhāṣya.* Two later commentators of Vyāsa's *Yoga-bhāṣya* are Vācaspati Miśra (9th cent.), to whom the gloss *Tattva-vaiśaradi* is attributed, and Vijñāna Bhikṣu (16th cent.), the author of *Yogasāra-saṁgraha.* King Bhoja's (beginning of 11th cent.) *Rājamārthanda* and Rāmānanda Sarasvati's (16th cent.) *Maṇiprabhā* are also counted as important commentaries.

c) Swami Prabhavananda's Commentary

Quotations from the *Yoga-sūtras* that are found in this chapter shall be from the translation by Swami Prabhavananda. In his translation he has taken the liberty to give a complete sentence structure where it is lacking in the original text. He has done so because he is a practical spiritual writer. A strictly literal version may not be intelligible to the reader. In order not to increase the already existing difficulties in the study of Patañjali he has tried to make it as intelligible as possible.

Swami Prabhavananda's work is also an interpretation of Patañjali. His commentary agrees with those of Vyāsa, Bhoja and Swami Vivekananda. Apart from his overconcern for Advaita,[4] Swami Prabhavananda's interpretation of Patañjali is deeply spiritual and intuitive. A spiritual vision is to be seen throughout the work. He can certainly claim to have presented a practical guide to spiritual life.

2. *Yoga in Indian Spirituality*

Yoga is one of the fundamental 'idea-forces' on which the whole of Indian spirituality rests.[5] From ancient times onwards it

---

[4] Swami Prabhavananda interprets Patañjali from an Advaita viewpoint (cf. SWAMI PRABHAVANANDA on *Yoga-sūtra,* p. viii). But his claim that prior to Patañjali Yoga was based on Advaita does not stand to reason. If Yoga was originally grounded on Advaita philosophy and if Patañjali dismembered it and grafted it on Sāṁkhya metaphysics, he must have done violence to the system itself. It is true that the Yoga disciplines were in existence at the time of some of the earliest Upaniṣads. It is also very probable that at the time of the Upaniṣads the Yoga disciplines were not associated with Sāṁkhya. But it is to be noted that according to both Sāṁkhya and Advaita the way to getting the liberating knowledge is a theoretic one; philosophico-religious inquiry is enough to dispel ignorance and to become conscious of the separation of Spirit from Nature in one case, and of the identity of the Self and Brahman in the other. Both of them considered that the Yoga disciplines were unnecessary. Śaṁkara in his commentary on the *Vedānta Sūtras of Bāḍarāyaṇa* II.i.3 openly refutes Yoga.

[5] Cf. MIRCEA ELIADE, *Le Yoga: Immortalité et Liberté* (Paris, 1954), p. 17.

was held in high esteem. To this day it remains as a specific dimension of Indian spirituality and mysticism.

In the Vedic period the word *yoga*[6] was used in many senses: yoking, harnessing, applying, connecting etc. The word *yuga* in the sense of 'yoke' was used in many texts. It was a word used by the agricultural Aryans. Slowly the meaning of 'yoking' began to cover the word.

In some ancient Upaniṣads one may find some allusions to Yoga. One passage in the Bṛhad-āraṇyaka Upaniṣad (BU 1.5.23) is an instruction regarding the inhaling and exhaling of breath as a means to win complete union with the divinity Breath. Another Upaniṣad (CU 8.15) asks the departing pupil to concentrate all his senses on the Self. But among the earlier Upaniṣads it is the Kaṭha Upaniṣad that comes closer to the classical sense of Yoga. This Upaniṣad mentions *adhyātma-yoga,* the yoking with one's essential self (KU 2. 12). It is the practice of self-contemplation, an effort to apprehend the Supreme in a way different from the ordinary way of knowledge. KU 6.10-11 is a definition of Yoga:

> v. 10: When cease the five
> [Sense-] knowledges, together with the mind (*manas*),
> And the intellect (*buddhi*) stirs not —
> That, they say, is the highest course.
> v. 11: This they consider as Yoga —
> The firm holding back of the senses.
> Then one becomes undistracted.
> Yoga, truly, is the origin and the end.

In v. 18 the Narrator says that the King of Death instructed Naciketas in the whole rule of Yoga, by which he attained Brahman and became free from passion and death.

Besides the Kaṭha Upaniṣad, systematic development of Yoga doctrines can be found in two other Upaniṣads of comparatively later period. They are the Śvetāśvatara and Maitrī Upaniṣads. It is also remarkable that these three Upaniṣads belong to the Black Yajur Veda. Clear references to Yoga are found only in them. The Śve-

---

Karman, māyā, nirvāṇa and *yoga* are the four key concepts of Indian spirituality. He says that based on these four concepts one can write a coherent history of Indian thought.

[6] There are two root forms for the word 'yoga': *yuj* and *yujir.* According to scholars 'yoga' means to discipline oneself, to exercise oneself. In the sense of 'yoking' it could mean both bringing the senses under control and also the joining with the Supreme Spirit.

tāśvatara Upaniṣad 2.8-14 give a detailed instruction on the practice of Yoga:

v. 8: Holding his body steady with the three [upper parts] erect,
And causing the senses with the mind to enter into the heart,
A wise man with the Brahma-boat should cross over
All the fear-bringing streams.

Here Yoga is a means for the attainment of knowledge of Brahman. The theory of posture is indebted to this verse for its later development. There is also a reference to the withdrawal of the senses.

v. 9: Having repressed his breathings here in the body, and having his movements checked,
One should breathe through his nostrils with diminished breath.
Like that chariot yoked with vicious horses,
His mind the wise man should restrain undistractedly.

This verse is an instruction regarding what is called control of breath, a practice which consists in the inhalation, exhalation, and retension of breath. Verse 10 stresses the importance of physical surroundings. Verse 11 is about the forms which gradually manifest Brahman. Verse 12 says that through concentration the yogi can experience the five subtle elements — earth, water, fire, air and space. Vv. 13-16 describe the four stages of Yoga, known as beginning (*ārambha*), intently occupied (*ghaṭa*), experience (*paricaya*) and maturity (*niṣpatti*). At the beginning of Yoga practice one begins to secure bodily health. In becoming free from grief, one enters the second stage. In the third stage one is released from all fetters. In the fourth stage the yogi realizes his identity with the Supreme Spirit.

By the time of the Maitrī Upaniṣad the techniques of Yoga meditation were developed. Vv. 18 and 19 of chapter 6 are devoted to the subject of Yoga. Verse 18 enumerates six limbs of Yoga. Of these, five pertain to the eight limbs of classical Yoga. They are: control of breath, withdrawal of the senses, meditation, concentration and enstasis. A new element, which is not in the *Yoga-sūtras,* is contemplative inquiry (*tarkaḥ*). The preliminary rules, observances and instructions regarding yogic postures have no place in the Maitrī Upaniṣad. This Upaniṣad as a whole has devoted a great part to the discussion on meditation.

Some of the Minor Upaniṣads of a much later period are so entirely devoted to the discussion on Yoga meditation, that they are often known as 'yogic Upaniṣads.' Of these Nādabindu, Yogatattva and Dhyānabindu Upaniṣads are rich store-houses of Yoga meditation.[7] The Nādabindu Upaniṣad personifies the mystical syllable OM and teaches how to meditate on it. The Yogatattva Upaniṣad mentions the eight limbs of Yoga. It divides Yoga into four classes: Mantra-yoga, Laya-yoga, Haṭha-yoga and Rāja-yoga. Obstacles to meditation are dealt with in this Upaniṣad, as well as some of the important meditative postures. The Dhyānbindu Upaniṣad has elaborate descriptions of the limbs of Yoga. It recognizes six of them.

Although the Gītā exposes the Yoga doctrines, we shall not treat them here because the Yoga taught by Kṛṣṇa is not the classical Yoga of Patañjali. It was rather a Yoga appropriated for the religious sect of the Bhagavatas.

We shall end this historical survey on the significance of Yoga in Indian spirituality here and say that from ancient times onwards Yoga was considered to be a specific characteristic of Indian mysticism. The spread of Yoga practices in ancient India was gradual and steady. Finally it took hold of Indian spirituality. There was a search for a spiritual experience, personal and concrete, which Yoga provided. Here is the secret of its success.

3. *The Philosophical Presuppositions of Yoga*

To understand Yoga we have to know what it presupposes. Generally Indologists treat Sāṁkhya and Yoga, two orthodox schools of Indian thought, as twin philosophies. The resemblances between them are mainly the following:

1. Both are dualistic. According to them Nature and Spirit are the only two ultimate principles.
2. The concept of liberation is the same. Isolation of Spirit from Nature is the goal of both schools.

There are also two essential differences between them:

1. Sāṁkhya is atheistic; Yoga admits the existence of God.
2. The method of salvation is different in both systems. According to Sāṁkhya isolation comes only through metaphysical knowledge;

[7] Other Upaniṣads belonging to this group are: Yogaśikha, Yogacūḍāmaṇi, Tejobindu, Amṛtānanda, Brahmabindu, Brahmavidya and Ksurika Upaniṣads.

Yoga, however, gives considerable importance to the techniques of meditation.[8]

We shall now examine Nature and Spirit, the two ultimate principles according to Sāṁkhya-Yoga.

a) Nature (*Prakṛti*)

In Patañjali's picture of the universe Nature is the primordial substance out of which the physical universe is evolved. She is the elemental, undifferentiated stuff of mind and matter. Mind, senses and ego are the modifications of Nature. She is the principle of all existence, the background of all phenomena. For Patañjali says: "Behind all subtle objects is Prakrti, the primal cause" (YS I. 45).

According to Swami Prabhavananda Nature is the power of Brahman.[9] Behind her is Brahman. Just as heat cannot exist separately from fire, so Nature does not have independent existence apart from Brahman. This tendency to identify her with the power of Brahman is a kind of compromise between Nature of Sāṁkhya and *māyā* of Advaita. By making her a power of Brahman, Advaita reduces the dualism of Sāṁkhya to non-dualism. Nature is similar to *māyā*. Just as *māyā,* she always changes. But she is eternal and real, *māyā* not.

Nature is dynamic and creative. But ultimately she remains incomprehensible by human intellect, which itself is under her sway.

b) Spirit (*Puruṣa*)

Nature does not exhaust the content of the universe. There is another principle, equally independent and eternal, Spirit. According to Swami Prabhavananda, it literally means "the Godhead that dwells within the body." [10]

Nature is only one; but there are many Spirits. The Spirit is static and inactive. It is the witness, isolated, indifferent seer.

Spirit's association with Nature is a mystery. The two appar-

---

8 On the question of the difference between Sāṁkhya and Yoga, scholars usually lay stress on Sāṁkhya atheism and Yoga theism. But a closer examination will demonstrate that Yoga theism is not very profound. The more fundamental difference between the two systems might be the different methods they employ in realizing final liberation.

9 Cf. Swami Prabhavananda on *Yoga-sūtra* I.17.

10 *Ibid.,* I.2.

ently contrary principles are made to co-operate. To Swami Prabhavananda this is a 'seeming paradox.'[11]

Yoga teaches that man's present state is a degeneration. The ignorance, which YS II.23-24 speak of, is one in which Spirit is entangled in an illusory relation with Nature. It is to consider what is noneternal (*anitya*), impure (*aśuci*), painful (*dukha*) and non-spirit (*anātma*) as eternal (*nitya*), pure (*śuci*), pleasant (*sukha*) and spirit (*ātma*) (YS II.5). This accounts for the whole misery of human existence.

Hence for Patañjali the problem is this: suffering is caused by ignorance of the true nature of Spirit (YS II.4,24). Man believes that his psycho-mental life is identical with Spirit (YS II.20). He confounds two realities entirely autonomous, even opposed. There is no true relation between them. For the psycho-mental experience does not belong to Spirit but to Nature. The latter produces the states of consciousness. The activity of senses, thoughts and desires — all are associated with her (YS I.45). She sets snares so that the Spirit may forsake its spiritual orientation. This is undesirable. Yoga's task is to eradicate this illusion. According to Patañjali liberation is the knowledge of this truth (YS I.26; II.25). It is isolation of Spirit from Nature (YS IV.34). It is to see through Nature and realize Spirit's absolute distinction from her (YS I.16; II.26). True, Sāṁkhya agrees with Yoga so far. But it is content with theoretical knowledge of the truth. Yoga wants to realize the truth. For this purpose it makes use of an experimental method. In its programme of the isolation of Spirit, the technique of meditation is found best suited. In the next two sections of this chapter we shall try to bring the different aspects of Yoga meditation to light. In the following section we shall deal with Patañjali's explanation of the limbs of Yoga. To understand Yoga meditation it is necessary to determine its place in the general context of Yoga.

C. The limbs of Yoga

Patañjali observed the nature of the mind. It wanders constantly. He then gave a number of instructions on the path of Yoga, beginning with self-purification and ending in perfect concentration of mind. In effect, they help man to move towards liberation. The

[11] Cf. *ibid.*, II.20-25.

eight courses are called eight parts of Yoga (*aṣṭāṅga-yoga*) or simply limbs of Yoga (*yogāṅga*).

Patañjali's detailed description of the limbs of Yoga appears in Book II:

> The eight limbs of yoga are: the various forms of abstention from evil-doing (yama), the various observances (niyamas), posture (asana), control of the prana, (pranayama), withdrawal of the mind from sense objects (pratyahara), concentration (dharana), meditation (dhyana) and absorption in the Atman (samadhi) (YS II.29).

Swami Prabhavananda considers the eight limbs important and justifies comment on them.[12] Each limb has a specific function. He puts them in a hierarchic order. He compares Yoga to a tree bearing luscious fruit: the two limbs of Yoga, abstention and observances, nourish the seed of Yoga tree. It is further fed by posture and control of breath. When it becomes a full-grown tree, it produces flowers of withdrawal of sense-objects. Its fruits are concentration, meditation and enstasis. We shall now see each limb in particular.

1. *Abstention* (*yama*)

Abstention is a course of conduct to remove the impurities of the mind. The mind is constantly moved by the thoughts of pleasure, injury, deception, possession and sex. The yogi must control these wild propensities by cultivating the opposite virtues. Swami Prabhavananda says that abstention is nothing special to Hinduism; it embraces the ethical disciplines universally taught by all the great religions.[13] There are five abstentions (YS II.30):

a) Non-injury (*ahiṁsā*) is considered to be the root of other abstentions. It is a great duty (*mahāvṛta*) to be practised always and everywhere.

In a negative sense non-injury means to cause no harm in dealing with others. Positively, it demands the cultivation of universal love. The idea of human solidarity is at its heart. In social relationships it fosters mutual respect; in religious circles it advocates tolerance.

b) Truthfulness (*satya*) is the sign of a well-balanced man. His words correspond to his mind. A truthful man sees the fulfilment of whatever he speaks.

---

[12] Cf. Swami Prabhavananda, SHI, p. 248.
[13] Cf. *ibid.*

Patañjali says:

> When a man becomes steadfast in his abstention from falsehood he gets the power of obtaining for himself and others the fruits of good deeds, without having to perform the deeds themselves (YS II.36).

Swami Prabhavananda comments on it:

> ... when a man becomes perfected in truthfulness, he gains control, so to speak, of the truth. He no longer has to "obey" facts; facts obey him. He cannot think or even dream a lie; everything he says becomes true. If he blesses someone, that person *is* blessed — no matter whether the blessing was deserved or not.[14]

c) Non-stealing (*asteya*). Abstention from theft is a remedy against attachment to things. Everything in the world belongs either to God or to Nature. To use such words as 'mine' or 'yours' is a kind of stealing. At best we are only borrowers.

d) Continence (*brahmacarya*). Next, Patañjali asks the yogi to control his sexual tendencies. Sexual activities use up a great portion of one's vital energy. Sexual energy can be sublimated as spiritual energy. According to Swami Prabhavananda it becomes transformed into spiritual energy when it is overcome.[15]

e) Non-coveteousness (*aparigraha*). To counteract avariciousness Patañjali demands non-receiving of gifts. Greed is inseparable from attachment; and attachment is an obstacle to spiritual knowledge.

Having explained the five abstentions, Patañjali now passes to the five observances which form the second limb of Yoga.

2. *Observances* (*niyama*) are characterized by the cultivation of positive virtues. They are: purity, contentment, austerity, study and devotion to God (YS II.32).

a) Purity (*śauca*) is cleanliness, both external and internal. Physical cleanliness is easier. The body is the temple of God. It is more important to keep the mind pure. The living presence of God has to be felt within the mind.

The result of purity is disgust at body (II.40), cheerfulness of mind, power of concentration, subjugation of senses and fitness to see the Spirit (YS II.41).

---

14 Swami Prabhavananda on *Yoga-sūtra* II.36.

15 Swami Prabhavananda, RP, p. 239.

b) Contentment (*saṁtoṣa*). The habit of contentment means calm acceptance of one's lot in life. It is neither passivity nor indifference, but a positive inner poise. Patañjali tells us that such a habit of contentment will result in supreme happiness (YS II.42).[16]

The remaining three observances form a single unity. They are called yoga of action.

c) Austerity (*tapaḥ*) is ascetic fervour. Swami Prabhavananda interprets it as the practice of conserving energy and directing it toward the goal of Yoga.[17] It is a means of destroying impurities of the mind (YS II.43). It renders the body docile to the exigencies of the Spirit.

d) Study (*svādhyāya*). Swami Prabhavananda interprets Patañjali's use of the term 'study' as not only the reading of the sacred scriptures but also the repetition of the name of God.[18] He recognizes three phases in the chanting of the sacred words: verbal, semi-verbal, and mental. The first is audible chanting; the second is the moving of the lips, without however, making any sound; in the third the sacred word is repeated only in mind.[19]

e) Devotion to God (*Īśvarapraṇidhāna*). In the present text (YS II.32) devotion to God means to work not for self, but for God.[20] Through it one becomes fit to reach enstasis.

Thus we see that the two preliminary limbs of Yoga — abstention and observances — do not make one specifically a yogi, but raise one to the state of a purified man. Purified by these physical and mental disciplines, he can now proceed to the third step.

3. *Posture* (*āsana*). The third limb of Yoga Patañjali calls posture. It means both the place which a yogi selects for his meditation and the manner in which he keeps his body. Regarding the first the Gītā says:

> Setting for himself in a pure place a firm seat neither very high nor very low, with a cloth, a deer-skin, and kuśa grass upon it (BG 6.11).

---

16 "The first sign of your becoming religious is that you are becoming cheerful." SWAMI VIVEKANANDA on *Yoga-sūtra* II.41. Swami Vivekananda's commentary on the *Yoga-sūtra* appears in: *The Complete Works of Swami Vivekananda* (Mayavati Memorial Edition, Almora, 1931⁵), Part I, pp. 117-313.

17 Cf. SWAMI PRABHAVANANDA on *Yoga-sūtra* II.1.

18 Cf. *ibid.,* II.44.

19 Cf. SWAMI PRABHAVANANDA, SHI, p. 250.

20 In Book I (YS I.23) devotion to God means love, homage and adoration to God as the one centre of meditation. In Book II (YS II. 1, 32, 45) it means the abnegation of all desires of the fruit of action to Him. Thus there is a remarkable difference in the use of the same expression in the two Books.

And regarding the second, the Gītā continues:

> Steady, holding his body, head, and neck balanced and motionless, fixing his gaze on the end of his nose, and looking not about him (BG 6.13).

What Patañjali said with regard to posture is very simple. The yogi is to sit firmly and relaxed (YS II.46). All that matters is to take a posture in which he can sit without strain, holding the chest, neck and head erect. Moreover Patanjali has spoken only with regard to the posture for meditation. From this rule Haṭha-yoga has elaborated various bodily postures. They have nothing to do with the posture as taught by Patañjali.

The traditional posture for meditation is the lotus-posture, in which the yogi sits cross-legged, with the feet drawn in to rest against the top of the thighs. At any rate a sitting position is recommended by all. *Vedānta Sūtras* IV.i.7-10 treat this question:

> Sitting (a man is to meditate), on account of the possibility. And on account of thoughtfulness. And with reference to immobility (scripture ascribes thought to the earth, & c.). And Smṛti-passages say the same.

Śaṁkara comments on this passage.[21] Since meditation is something mental why should there be any restriction as to the position of the body? He answers that meditation is the lengthened carrying on of an identical train of thought and that such thoughtfulness is easy for those who sit. He thus concludes that a sitting posture subserves the act of meditation.

The purpose of posture is to be freed from physical tensions during meditation. A steady and comfortable posture helps to keep equilibrium of the mind. It controls the body and nervous system. Swami Prabhavananda sees another value of holding the body erect. One thinks more clearly in that position than when one is sitting with a bent back. When the mind of a yogi is deeply absorbed a spiritual current is felt in the spinal column. For spiritual benefit this spiritual power has to pass through a central channel called *suṣumna.* The passage to it is likely to remain closed in a person sitting with a bent back.[22]

---

[21] Cf. *Śaṁkara Bhāṣya on Vedānta Sūtras* IV.i.7ff.

[22] Cf. SWAMI PRABHAVANANDA on *Yoga-sūtra* II.46.

4. *Control of the Prāṇa* (*prāṇāyāma*)

Earlier in YS 1.34 Patañjali spoke of the control of *prāṇa* as a means to calm the mind. *Prāṇa* means vital breath — the life-force that enables us to act, to think, to breathe. It is the primal energy or the life-principle of the whole universe. The one cosmic energy moves man as well. The ancient sages recognized this life-giving principle. For example, the Praśna Upaniṣad dedicates Questions 1 to 3 to the explanation of this vital energy.[23]

Prāṇāyāma is the control of this energy. Mastery over breathing in and out can be gained by practice. It establishes harmony between body and the mind. The principle may be stated thus: body and mind are mutually influential; actions and reactions of the one affect the other. This principle was known to the yogis of India from an immemorial past. Deep and steady breathing is a sign of mental equilibrium; irregular breathing indicates passions and mental disturbances.

But *prāṇāyāma* is merely a physical means to a spiritual end. Swami Prabhavananda explains the reason why he refrains from giving the breathing exercises in his books. What is taught by Patañjali is radically different from the breathing exercises belonging to the Haṭha-yoga school. He claims to have personal knowledge of instances in which breathing exercises without the guidance of an adept teacher have proved to be of great danger.[24]

5. *Withdrawal of Sense-objects* (*pratyāhāra*)

Most distractions come from the mind's attachment to sense-objects. Swami Prabhavananda compares the mind to a monkey — mad, drunk and stung by a scorpion.[25] The naturally restless mind, drunk with the wine of desires, stung by the scorpion of passions, is to be checked. Generally the powers of the mind are scattered and dissipated. The yogi has to carefully gather in the forces of the mind.

---

[23] The controversy between *prāṇa* and the organs of sense appears in the Upaniṣads in different manner. Cf. Praśna U 2.3-4; CU 5.1.6-15; BU 6.1.7-14.

[24] The only kind of breathing exercise Swami Prabhavananda recommends is as follows: close the right nostril with the thumb of the right hand and through the left nostril breathe in; then expel the air through the right nostril, closing the left. Again inhale through the right nostril, repeating the process in reverse. By this exercise one may attain purity of the nerves. Cf. SWAMI PRABHAVANANDA, SHI, p. 253 n. 1.

[25] Cf. *ibid.*, p. 254.

The five limbs of Yoga described above are called external aids to Yoga (*bahiräṅga-sādhanā*). The remaining three are called internal ones (*antaraṅga-sādhanā*) and are more important. They are concentration, meditation and enstasis. To these three Patañjali gives a technical name — *saṁyama* (YS III.4). Literally it means 'to go together.' It exists when concentration, meditation and enstasis are in one, one following the other and making the whole a single process. The three represent three stages of the same process. We shall now consider each in particular.

6. *Concentration* (*dhāraṇa*) is defined by Patañjali as

> ... holding the mind within a center of spiritual consciousness in the body, or fixing it on some divine form, either within the body or outside it (YS III.1).

Earlier in Book I in a series of rules (YS I.17-20; 23; 32; 35-40) Patañjali had already introduced the idea of concentration, giving its division (17-18) and the ways of cultivating it (35-40). But there it was spoken of in relation to calming the mind (2-4). In Book III he speaks of it for another purpose, namely to comprehend the object concentrated upon.

Dhāraṇa comes from the root *dhṛ-*, to keep a tight hold (on something). It is the vigilant keenness spoken of in one Upaniṣad.[26] In defining concentration as fixing the mind on a single point, Patañjali asks the yogi to have undivided attention on a particular object, be it physical or mental. Vyāsa explains it:

> Binding of mind-stuff, only in so far as it is a fluctuation, to the navel or to the heart-lotus or to the light within the head or to the tip of the nose or to the tip of the tongue or to other places of the same kind or to an external object, — this is fixed-attention (dhāraṇa).[27]

Such concentration is called *ekāgratā* (only one point).

---

[26] Kaṭha Upaniṣad 3.12:
Though He is hidden in all things,
That Soul (Ātman, Self) shines not forth.
But he is seen by subtle seers
With superior, subtle intellect.

Śrī Rāmakṛṣṇa gives two examples of concentration: a hunter aiming at a bird and a man angling fish in a lake. Cf. *Gospel*, pp. 720-21.

[27] VYĀSA, *Yoga-bhāṣya* III.1. Vyāsa's commentary on the *Yoga-sūtra* is translated by James Haughton Woods in his: *The Yoga-System of Patañjali* (Harward Oriental Series Vol. XVII. The Harward University Press, 1927).

In Book I Patañjali mentions a few objects of concentration. They are OM (I.28), the inner Light (I.36), the heart of a holy personality (I.37) or a dream experience (I.38). According to Yoga there is no uniform method of concentration. Patañjali is suggesting only some general forms (I.39). Each spiritual aspirant has to find out the method proper to him with the help of his *guru.*

Swami Prabhavananda emphasizes the importance of concentration on the 'lotus of the heart.' Yoga recognizes seven centres of spiritual consciousness. The first three are located within the spine. The fourth is in the heart; the fifth is near the throat; the sixth is between the eyebrows. And finally the seventh is at the tip of the head. Of these the heart centre is the most important. Swami Prabhavananda explains:

> The ancient yogis believed that there was an actual center of spiritual consciousness, called "the lotus of the heart," situated between the abdomen and the thorax, which could be revealed in deep meditation. They claimed that it had the form of a lotus and that it shone with an inner light. It was said to be "beyond sorrow," since those who saw it were filled with an extraordinary sense of peace and joy.[28]

It is in connection with a mystical imagination that the idea of lotus is associated to the heart centre. Accordingly, there is a lotus flower with eight petals. Before the time of meditation the lotus remains a bud, with petals closed. At the time of meditation it blooms. For there shines a sun inside the lotus; within the sun shines the moon; within the moon is the fire. The object of meditation is within the fire.

The Upaniṣads instruct:

> Enter the lotus of the heart and there meditate on the presence of Brahman — the pure, the blissflul (Kaivalya U 6).
> *Om!* [The teacher should say:] 'Now, what is here in this city of Brahma, is an abode, a small lotus-flower. Within that is a small space. What is within that, should be searched out; that, assuredly, is what one should desire to understand' (CU 8.1.1).
> 'As far, verily, as this world-space (*ayam ākāśa*) extends, so far extends the space within the heart. Within it, indeed, are contained both heaven and earth, both fire and wind, both sun and moon, lightning and the stars, both what one possesses here and what one does not possess; everything here is contained within it' (CU 8.1.3).

---

[28] SWAMI PRABHAVANANDA on *Yoga-sūtra* I.36.

In order to concentrate, the yogi may fix his mind upon this mystically imagined lotus as located within his own body. The Hindu tradition has also other methods of concentration. In Viṣṇu Purāṇa Keśidhvaja instructs Khāṇḍikya on the object of concentration:

> ... let him [the sage] resolutely effect the fixation of his mind upon that receptacle of all the three energies (Vishṇu), for that is the operation of the mind which is called perfect Dhāraṇā ... The retention or apprehension by the mind of that visible form of Vishṇu, without regard to subsidiary forms, is thence called Dhāraṇā; and I will describe to you the perceptible form of Hari, which no mental retention will manifest, except in a mind that is fit to become the receptacle of the idea. The meditating sage must think (he beholds internally the figure) of Vishṇu as having a pleased and lovely countenance, with eyes like the leaf of the lotus, smooth cheeks, and a broad and brilliant forehead, ears of equal size, the lobes of which are decorated with splendid pendants; a painted neck, and a broad breast, on which shines the Śrīvatsa mark; a belly falling in graceful folds, with a deep-seated navel; eight long arms, or else four; and firm and well-knit thighs and legs, with well-formed feet and toes. Let him, with well-governed thoughts, contemplate, as long as he can persevere in unremitting attention, Hari as clad in a yellow robe, wearing a rich diadem on his head, and brilliant armlets and bracelets on his arms, and bearing in his hands the bow, the shell, the mace, the sword, the discus, the rosary, the lotus, and the arrow. When this image never departs from his mind, whether he be going or standing, or be engaged in any other voluntary act, then he may believe his retention to be perfect.[29]

When the yogi has succeeded in holding his mind on any one of the spiritual centres of consciousness, he can proceed to the next limb called meditation.

7. *Meditation* (*dhyāna*). "Meditation is prolonged concentration." [30]

The object of concentration remains the same in meditation. Meditation is understood as the continuance in the object of concentration. Patañjali defines it as "an unbroken flow of thought toward the object of concetration" (YS II.2).

When, in perfect concentration, the yogi can send a current of unified thought in a single direction for a certain length of time, he can be said to have reached the state of meditation. What Vyāsa says on meditation is important. For him meditation is:

---

[29] *Viṣṇu Purāṇa* 6.7, trans. Horace Hayman Wilson (Calcutta, 1961[3] = First Edition, London, 1840).

[30] SWAMI PRABHAVANANDA on *Yoga-sūtra* III.2.

> The focusedness [31] of the presented idea upon the subject to be contemplated in that place, in other words, the stream [of presented ideas] of like quantity unaffected by any other presented idea.[32]

Even more important is Vijñāna Bhikṣu's comment on the process of meditation [33]: when the mind has reached perfect concentration, there is a flow of the activity of the mind in the form of the object of meditation, unimpeded by any other function, the process constitutes meditation. As examples of such unimpeded flow of thought, he refers to a meditation of the Four-armed (Viṣṇu), imagined to be present in the lotus of the heart; the meditation on the Thinking Principle of Intelligence (*Caitanya*); or the meditation of the Lord in the Causal Condition (*Karaṇopādhi*).

The distance between concentration and meditation is short. With the deepening of concentration the yogi reaches meditation. Swami Vivekananda explains it in this way: the mind thinks of one object. If it succeeds in receiving sensations only through that part of the body it is called concentration. When the mind keeps itself in that state for some time it is meditation.[34]

Swami Prabhavananda interprets YS III.2 from the general outlook of Yoga philosophy. Patañjali defines Yoga as the suppression of the thought-waves in the mind (YS I.2). Thought in Yoga psychology is a wave of the mind. Ordinarily a thought-wave comes, remains for a moment, and then sinks down. It is followed by another. In this case there is a discontinuance. Meditation creates a perfect continuity of the thought-waves of the mind. If the same wave is repeated in the mind, identical thought succeeds each other. Swami Prabhavananda says of its process:

> In the practice of meditation, a succession of identical waves is raised in the mind; and this is done so quickly that no one wave is allowed to subside before another rises to take its place. The effect is therefore one of perfect continuity.[35]

To explain the state of meditation he uses an illustration. The steadiness of the mind in meditation can be compared to shooting a hundred feet of film without moving either the camera or the object.

---

[31] Focusedness means singleness-of-intent.

[32] Vyāsa, *Yoga-bhāṣya* III.2.

[33] Cf. Vijñāna Bhikṣu, *Yogasāra-saṁgraha.* E.T. with Sanskrit Text. Trans. Ganganatha Jha (Bombay, 1894), § 44.

[34] Cf. Swami Vivekananda on *Yoga-sūtra* III.2.

[35] Swami Prabhavananda on *Yoga-sūtra* III.2.

The result is a still photograph as it were. The many identical pictures become as if one. In the same way, the mind remains steady in Yoga meditation. It is an experience of a true integration of the mental power of a man.

According to Swami Prabhavananda the meditation of a yogi differs radically from what is usually understood by the term.[36] The Christian concept generally implies the absorption of the mind in a subject, with all the ideas connected with it. Thus it is more or less a discursive operation of the mind. The yogic idea of meditation, on the contrary, is to prevent multiplicity of thoughts from arising in the mind and to let flow an uninterrupted current of thought to the exclusion of everything else. He holds that the Christian idea of meditation is only preliminary to Yoga meditation.

8. *Enstasis* (*samādhi*). Now Patañjali describes enstasis, the ultimate limb of Yoga:

> When, in meditation, the true nature of the object shines forth, not distorted by the mind of the perceiver, that is absorption (samadhi) (YS III.3).

Vyāsa gives the following explanation:

> When the contemplation (dhyāna) only shines forth [in consciousness] in the form of the object-to-be contemplated and [so] is, as it were, empty of itself, in so far as it becomes identical with the presented-idea as such, then, by fusing [itself] with the nature of the object-to-be-contemplated, it is said to be concentration (samādhi).[37]

Enstasis shows the final stage of the process begun with concentration. It is the consummation and crown of innumerable acts of concentration and meditation.[38] It signifies union in totality, total concentration of the mind or union with the object of meditation. It is the state of Yoga which a yogi achieves when his meditation deepens and his mind is transformed into the object of meditation. His mind becomes one with the object by intense concentration and meditation and the process continues, to the exclusion of all other thoughts.

Patañjali describes enstasis as the state in which true knowledge results (YS III.3). The knowledge in enstasis differs from all other

---

36 Cf. *ibid.*

37 Vyāsa, *Yoga-bhāṣya* III.3.

38 Cf. M. Eliade, *Le Yoga: Immortalité et Liberté*, p. 93.

knowledge.[39] The Viṣṇu Purāṇa brings out this characteristic knowledge in enstasis:

> This process of forming a lively image in the mind, exclusive of all other objects, constitutes Dhyāna, or meditation, which is perfected by six stages: and when an accurate knowledge of self, free from all distinction, is attained by this mental meditation, that is termed Samādhi.[40]

By "free from all distinction" is understood, a distinction between the object of meditation and the meditation itself. Enstasis is free from this distinction.

The main stress of Yoga seems to be on its method of enstasis. Intense meditation purifies the mind. The mind, made pure, becomes so immersed in the object of concentration that it loses itself in it. It has no awareness of itself. The object alone remains. Vijñāna Bhikṣu notes that when meditation becomes free from all ideas of meditation, its object and the meditant, and subsists in the form of the object of meditation in its absolute purity, the yogi is said to have reached the state of enstasis.[41] In the Viṣṇu Purāṇa Keśidhvaja, after having instructed Khāṇḍikya on the eight aids to Yoga, sums up by saying:

> Embodied spirit is the user of the instrument, which instrument is true knowledge; and by it that (identification) of the former (with Brahma) is attained. Liberation, which is the object to be effected, being accomplished, discriminative knowledge ceases.[42]

The individual spirit has thinking as the means to liberation. When it has completed its task, it disappears.

There are two important differences between meditation and enstasis. The first is with regard to the specification of time. In meditation the idea of time is not altogether abolished. In enstasis, on the other hand, the idea of time ceases to exist. "The mind becomes one-pointed when similar thought-waves arise in succession without any gaps between them" (YS III.12). The second is with

---

[39] After explaining the ordinary way of knowledge, S. Dasgupta writes: "Knowledge or ordinary perception is limited by the incapacity of our senses to perceive subtle and remote things, and things which are obstructed from our view. But Samādhi has no such limitations, so the knowledge that can be attained by it is absolutely unobstructed, true and real in the strictest sense of the terms." S. Dasgupta, *The Study of Patañjali* (University of Calcutta, 1920), p. 169.

[40] *Viṣṇu Purāṇa* vi.7.

[41] Cf. Vijñāna Bhikṣu, *Yogasāra-saṁgraha,* § 44.

[42] *Viṣṇu Purāṇa* vi.7.

regard to the perception of objects during meditation. Meditation is broken up when the senses of the aspirant happen to come in contact with objects. In enstasis he knows nothing, either external or internal.

We have so far described enstasis in general. Patañjali and commentators admit mainly two stages of enstasis: (1) the conscious enstasis (*samprajñāta samādhi*) and (2) the unconscious enstasis (*asamprajñāta samādhi*). According to Vijñāna Bhikṣu the former is that in which the object of enstasis is properly perceived.[43] That is to say, it is the suppression of all functions of the thinking principle, save the one related to the object of enstasis. The principal characteristic of conscious enstasis consists in its being the suppression of the functions of the thinking principle, preceded by the direct perception of the object of enstasis.

In Book I Patañjali gives a number of rules (YS I.41-44) which give a division of enstasis. Accordingly conscious enstasis has many stages: *vitarka, vicāra, ānanda* and *asmitā*. The first two are further divided into *savitarka* and *nirvitarka, savicāra* and *nirvicāra*.

1. *Savitarka* means 'argumentative.' It is the lowest stage of enstasis. Through intense concentration on an object the mind may become identified with it; yet it retains the characteristics of ordinary consciousness, which according to Patañjali is "mixed with awareness of name, quality and knowledge" (YS I.42). The mind seems to become one with the meditated object together with its name and concept. This kind of enstasis comes from concentration on a thing in its gross aspect, the most external order of phenomena.

2. *Nirvitarka* means 'non-argumentative.' Here too the object of concentration is in its gross aspect. But it differs from the former one in so far as it is "unmixed with awareness of name, quality and knowledge" (YS I.43). The mind becomes one with the object of concentration, without any consciousness of its name and qualities. Memory stops functioning; knowledge comes as if in a super-rational experience. This is real knowledge, knowledge of the "thing-in-itself." [44]

3. *Savicāra* is 'deliberative.' Here the mind dwells no more on the exterior aspect of material objects, but on what Sāṁkhya and Yoga call *tanmātra,* the subtle essence within. The mind ident-

---

[43] Cf. Vijñāna Bhikṣu, *Yogasāra-saṁgraha* § 4.
[44] Swami Prabhavananda on *Yoga-sūtra* I.43.

ifies itself with these. But here again the consciousness is accompanied by the notion of time and space.

4. *Nirvicāra,* 'non-deliberative,' is the indeterminate subtle enstasis. It has no notion even of time and space. The mind, now completely purified, is in a state of final seclusion.

Higher than these are the *ānanda* and the *asmitā* states.

5. In the *ānanda* (bliss) state there is a peculiar perception in the form of pleasure. The mind concentrates on the intellect and the senses. These arouse pleasure.

6. In the *asmitā* (sense of ego) state the perception is in the form: 'I am other than my body.' It is a state of pure existence, a simple awareness of individuality.

These are the different stages in the mind's becoming one with the object. In all these stages there are objects to which the mind consciously unites itself. Therefore they are called the conscious types of enstasis. Patañjali calls them also enstasis "with seed" (*bījasamādhi*) (YS I.46). It is a means to isolation in so far as it renders possible the comprehension of the truth regarding the Spirit. When the different states of conscious enstasis have been experienced, the yogi reaches the last stage of enstasis called the unconscious (*asamprajñāta* or *nirodha*) enstasis.

According to Vijñāna Bhikṣu this type of enstasis means that in which all consciousness disappears.[45] Consciousness returns to its source. There are no more thought-waves in the mind. The mind passes into a state of pure vacuum; it becomes absolutely contentless. All its potencies being destroyed, the mind goes back to Nature, its source, never again to bind the Spirit. Patañjali says:

> When the impression made by that samadhi is also wiped out, so that there are no more thought-waves at all in the mind, then one enters the samadhi which is called "seedless" (YS I.51).

The past impressions also become unproductive like burnt seeds (YS I.18). The mind is restored to its original luminosity in which the true nature of the Spirit is revealed (YS I.41). It realizes that there is no difference between itself and the Spirit. This is 'real knowledge' (*Tattva-jñāna*). This state is one of total integration of the Spirit in its spiritual essence. It is called isolation (*kaivalya*) in which the Spirit realizes its absolute separation from Nature. There is

---

45 Cf. Vijñāna Bhikṣu, *Yogasāra-saṁgraha* § 5.

no consciousness of 'I' or 'mine.' This is a spiritual experience of the highest order. Vācaspati Miśra says: 'the fruit of samprajñāta is asamprajñāta, and the fruit of the latter is kaivalya.'[46]

Swami Prabhavananda's interpretation of enstasis is highly illuminating. But after a critical examination we note a few points: His commentary on conscious enstasis is according to classical Yoga.[47] Passing to unconscious enstasis, he tries to interpret it in terms of Advaita.[48] He introduces the discussion saying that it is "the ultimate step into complete union with Brahman."[49] In the discussion itself he speaks not exactly of it but of *nirvikalpa samādhi.* This he does presumably because he thinks that all spiritual experiences are ultimately the same. Here we have to disagree with him. For the idea of liberation according to Advaita and Yoga is different: in the former the liberated self is merged into Brahman; in the latter the liberated Spirit retains individuality as pure intelligence. In the one case it is union of the individual self with the Supreme Self; in the other it is complete aloofness of Spirit from Nature (YS IV.34).

D. The Yoga meditation

Having seen the place of meditation in the general outlook of the Yoga system, we now come to the last part of this chapter which deals specifically with Yoga meditation.

1. *Yoga - A Training for Meditation?*

Swami Prabhavananda says that in order to understand Patañjali's technique of meditation, it is necessary to have a clear knowledge of the theory of evolution.[50] Therefore we have to examine briefly the Hindu doctrine of evolution.

Evolution in Sāṁkhya-Yoga is the development (*sṛṣṭi*) of the categories of existence. The heterogeneous universe is evolved out of the homogeneous Nature; and it is said to go back into her. To

---

46 Cf. Vācaspati Miśra, *Tattvavaiśaradi* I.21. Translation of this commentary on the *Yoga-bhāṣya* is taken from J. H. Woods' *The Yoga-System of Patañjali.* See n. 27, above.

47 Cf. Swami Prabhavananda on *Yoga-sūtra* I.41-44.

48 Cf. *ibid.,* I.51.

49 *Ibid.,* I.50.

50 Cf. *ibid.,* 1.17.

explain the universe, creation 'ex nihilo' is not admitted. The present universe is neither the first nor the last; it is only one of a series. The history of the universe is only the history of many evolutions. In the process of evolution nothing new is added. In other words, evolution is the gradual transformation of what exists potentially in the cause.

Nature, the elemental, undifferentiated primordial matter, does not evolve by herself. She is an eternal principle. How, then, does the universe evolve from her? She is composed of three elements, *sattva, rajas* and *tamas,* which are collectively known as 'strands' (*guṇa*). These pass through phases of equilibrium and disturbance. As long as they maintain their equilibrium, evolution remains only in a potential state. As soon as the balance is destroyed, evolution begins to take place. The strands always unite, separate and unite again, with one strand predominant in a thing and the others remaining latent. In this way there is a variety of objects in the universe.

Hence, it is the interaction of the strands which provokes evolution. Evolution is realized by stages. The following diagram may be helpful to understand the stages of evolution.

P R A K Ṛ T I

1. *Mahat* (the great cause, the pure mind-stuff)
↓
2. *Buddhi* (the intellectual faculty)
↓
3. *Ahaṁkāra* (sense of ego)
↓

↓	↓	↓	↓
4. *Manas* (memory-faculty) —	5-9 Five powers of perception: sight, hearing, smell, taste, touch —	10-14 Five organs of action: tongue, feet, hands, organs of evacuation & procreation —	15-19 Five subtle principles (*tanmātrās*) subtle inner essences of: sight, sound, smell, taste, touch ↓ 20-24 Five gross elements: ether, air, fire, water, earth

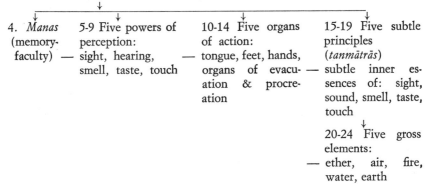

These twenty-four categories make up the universe. Summing up this explanation of the doctrine of evolution, Swami Prabhavananda considers that it is an outward development, "from undifferentiated into differentiated consciousness, from mind to matter." [51] Pure consciousness (such as Spirit), is slowly covered by successive layers of ignorance and differentiation, each layer being more material than the one below it, until the process ends on the outer physical surface of the universe.

Now we can better understand Swami Prabhavananda's advice to keep a clear idea of evolution in mind in order to understand Patañjali's technique of meditation. "For meditation is evolution in reverse." [52] Evolution is an outward process. It begins with the strands losing their equilibrium, continues with the arrangement of new stages and ends with the visible universe. Just the opposite is the direction of meditation. The meditant begins with the outward and proceeds to the inward. The thought-waves are the projections of the strands. One has to transcend them. This is being done in meditation. By focusing the mind entirely on the one object of meditation, a perfect continuity of the thought-waves is effected. The meditant creates a great thought-wave which swallows up all the rest. In this way the tendency of the strands to destroy the equilibrium is impeded. Beginning at the gross elements, the most external phenomena, the meditant proceeds to the less material, till at last the self-revelation of the Spirit is made. This, then, is the technique of meditation proposed by Patañjali. Swami Prabhavananda explains:

> It is necessary to keep this idea of evolution clearly in mind if we are to understand Patanjali's technique of meditation. For meditation is evolution in reverse. Meditation is a process of devolution. Beginning at the surface of life, the meditative mind goes inward, seeking always the cause behind the appearance, and then the cause behind the cause, until the innermost Reality is reached.[53]

2. *Who are Fit for Yoga Meditation?*

In showing the path of meditation, Patañjali had in mind a definite goal: the liberation of the Spirit from its empirical condition which consists in the Spirit's becoming aware of itself and separating itself from Nature. For this purpose he proposes a threefold method, physiological, mental and mystic. Yoga prescribes solitude, absolute

---

[51] *Ibid.*
[52] *Ibid.*
[53] *Ibid.*

chastity, withdrawal of senses from their objects etc. All these prohibit exactly what the human nature is inclined to do. Hence it is natural that all people are not prepared for Yoga meditation.

Commentators of *Yoga-bhāṣya* have differently classified the candidates for Yoga meditation. We give here Bhoja's classification since Swami Prabhavananda follows his explanation. Bhoja, according to Swami Prabhavananda, discovers five classes of mind: [54]

1. Scattered mind (*ṣipra citta*) is "restless, passionate and unable to concentrate." [55] It is tossed up and down by the constant rise of passions. Hence such a mind lacks self-mastery and concentration.

2. Dull mind (*mūdha citta*) is the victim of darkness. It is lazy, inert and consequently incapable of constructive thought.

3. Occasionally steady mind (*viṣipra citta*) is very often distracted. At times it is restless and at other times calm. It avoids the painful duties and selects only the pleasurable.

None of these three types of mind can attain the Yoga meditation. The following two kinds of mind are predominated by goodness.

4. One-pointed mind (*ekāgra citta*) is concentrated. It is ready for receiving knowledge.

5. Restrained mind (*nirūdha citta*) is pure and tranquil. Passions do not agitate it. There are no mental modifications. Such a mind is easily led to isolation.

In many people the ordinary mental states have a preponderance either of passion or of darkness. When the ordinary mental state stops functioning, the mind flows with an abundance of goodness. Every mind, no matter what its present condition, can become one-pointed and restrained and dispose itself for meditation.

---

[54] Cf. SWAMI PRABHAVANANDA, SHI, pp. 238-239. Vijñāna Bhikṣu speaks of three types of aspirants for yogic meditation — low, medium and high. They are:
1. *Āruruksu* — one attempting to climb the steps of meditation.
2. *Yunjāna* — one who is engaged in the practice of meditation. These two classes are beginners. According to him Patañjali prescribes the five abstentions and the five observances to these, in order that they may reach the interior purification and rise to the higher yoga practices.
3. *Yogārudha* — one who has already risen to the heights of meditation. To them are proposed only practice (*abhyāsa*) and detachment (*vairāgya*). Cf. VIJÑĀNA BHIKṢU, *Yogasāra-saṁgraha* § 22.

[55] SWAMI PRABHAVANANDA on *Yoga-sūtra* I.2.

How can this be achieved?

Patañjali gives the rules of conduct in a general way:

> The concentration of the true spiritual aspirant is attained through faith, energy, recollectedness, absorption and illumination (YS I.20).

The first requirement is faith. Swami Prabhavananda compares it to a plant which keeps on throwing forth shoots and growing.[56] Faith in the course taken by the yogi removes his fears and anxieties. Real faith has an impetus to act. This is what Patañjali calls energy or spiritual strenuousness (*vīrya*). When faith increases and strenuousness follows it, the mind becomes 'recollected.' Usually the mental powers are scattered. Now they take a unified direction, the object of meditation. In practising this, the mind becomes absorbed in the thought of what it is seeking (i. e., enstasis). Finally there comes wisdom, the right knowledge about the true nature of Spirit and Nature.

Again, in order to prepare the mind for meditation, the yogi has to overcome the physical and mental obstacles enumerated in YS I.30-31. They prevent the mind from being steady. To remove them Patañjali advises to practise "contemplation upon a single truth" (YS I.32). Although he simply stresses the importance of single-mindedness, Swami Prabhavananda interprets the 'single truth' as the "truth of God's existence."[57] Thought of God is efficacious in purifying the mind. In this manner even the lowest class of aspirants can equip themselves for the practice of meditation. Their earnestness will eventually qualify them to undertake Yoga meditation.

3. *The Yoga Meditation*

Scholars generally distinguish three main stages in the Yoga meditation:[58] bodily discipline, repetition of a sacred formula, concentration on God in order to become like Him. In the first stage the yogi is concerned with the control of his body. The ideal is to be devoid of the consciousness of possessing a body. Special attention is paid with regard to the selection of the place for meditation. The Kaivalya Upaniṣad 5 and the Bhagavad-Gītā 6.10 suggest a solitary place. The place of meditation should be quiet

---

[56] Cf. *ibid.,* I.20.

[57] *Ibid.,* 1.32.

[58] Cf. M. Dhavamony, "Hindu Meditation," in: *Studia Missionalia,* 25 (1976) 139.

and free from disturbances. In ancient times mountain peaks and forests were selected. The yogi takes a firm but relaxed posture. Traditional preference was the so-called lotus-posture; but it is not an absolute requirement. Holding the body erect, but without strain, the yogi may be able to forget the body altogether. Another great obstacle to concentration and meditation is the respiratory process. The yogis have found out a way to stop it. It is a method of breathing-in, keeping the breath for a while and then breathing-out. With practice one may be able to retain the breath for a long time. When there is no need of constant respiratory action, one of the main obstacles is surpassed.

When the body is thus brought under perfect control, the yogi can proceed to the second stage. Its aim is the purification of the mind. The ethical disciplines, discussed in the last section, are valuable means to this end. Repetition of a sacred formula is also a very effective means to make the mind pure. After a careful training of the mind, the mind must become free from all selfish attachments and disinclined to all worldly pleasures. At this stage meditation begins.

The last stage of Yoga meditation is a threefold process in one, concentration-meditation-enstasis. They are direct aids to experience (YS III.7). The yogi fixes his mind on any object of his choice. It is, however, beneficial to fix the attention on God. There is no special technique to pass from concentration to meditation. It is enough to repeat the same thought constantly in the mind. Patañjali says:

> The mind becomes one-pointed when similar thought-waves arise in succession without any gaps between them (YS III.12).

When the mind is concentrated on one object to the exclusion of others, and that for a considerable length of time, the mind is said to have reached meditation. It is the same thought and not successive thoughts, that is made to rise continuously in the mind. According to the yogis the time needed for a concentration is twelve seconds. If the mind can persist in that concentration for twelve times twelve seconds (i. e., two minutes and twenty-four seconds), one gets yogic meditation. If the mind can continue in that meditation for twelve times two minutes and twenty-four seconds (i. e., twenty-eight minutes and forty-eight seconds), this is a lower enstasis. And if the lower one can be maintained for twelve times that period

(i. e., five hours, forty-five minutes and thirty-six seconds), this reaches the higher enstasis.[59]

During meditation the mind becomes absorbed in the consciousness of the object of meditation. Slowly it becomes steady. Perfect tranquillity takes possession of it. As meditation deepens, the mind is transformed and becomes one with its object, just as a pure crystal assumes the colour of whatever object it is placed near. Then the mind is entirely freed from any other thought. There exists no consciousness of any difference between the meditator, the object of meditation and meditating. This is called enstasis. We have already described its six stages.[60] They are different stages of the lower enstasis in so far as they carry with them consciousness of the object of meditation.

At a certain stage of deep concentration on an object, the yogi may find himself endowed with psychic power (*vibhūti*).[61] They are the greatest stumbling block to spiritual life, since there is a terrible temptation to misuse them for motives of personal greed and ambition. The yogi, who is true to his ideal of spiritual life, pays no heed to them. For:

> They are powers in the worldly state, but they are obstacles to samadhi (YS III. 38).
> By giving up even these powers, the seed of evil is destroyed and liberation follows (YS III.51).

The greatest power, therefore, is to overcome these powers themselves.

The powers come to strengthen the faith and hope in Yoga. At last the yogi enters the state called unconscious enstasis, the highest

---

59 Cf. Swami Prabhavananda on *Yoga-sūtra* III.9ff.

60 See above, pp. 74-75.

61 In Book III.16 onwards Patañjali begins to describe the occult powers. In all they are nineteen. Swami Prabhavananda compares Christ's miracles to these and says that they can be developed by all people. The psychic powers are said to happen as a result of the mind's union with the object. The law of cause and effect does not apply to the particular object of yogi's concentration. Swami Prabhavananda's attitude to the psychic powers deserves special mention. He translates the sūtras dealing with them only for the sake of completeness and makes no comments or as little as possible. He compares them to cocaine which, in the hands of a responsible doctor, is a beneficial pain-killer and in the hands of an addict, a disaster. Occult powers are used by a saint with discrimination and without temptations of ego. He refers to the examples of Christ, who rejected their use for unspiritual ends. Cf. Swami Prabhavananda on *Yoga-sūtra* I.17; III.16, 51. Cf. also Id., SHI, p. 258.

illumination. It is a state in which there exists a complete "cessation of all waves of the mind" (YS I.2). By remaining long in this state the impressions created by the continued experience of worldly cares are destroyed. At this stage ordinary consciousness is totally surpassed and the mind exists in its own true infinite aspect. Now there dawns the true knowledge (*prajñā*). This spiritual wisdom comes to the yogi in seven stages. We shall paraphrase here Swami Prabhavananda's interpretation of the seven stages.[62]

The first stage is the conviction that true knowledge is not to be sought elsewhere but in the Spirit. This convincing realization puts an end to suffering. With the spiritual illumination in enstasis the third and fourth stages are reached and in different degrees of intensity. The fifth stage is named in Sanskrit *kārya vimukti,* liberation through individual effort. This is followed by *citta vimukti* which is the process of release of the Spirit from mind-stuff. Lastly, the true knowledge of the nature of the Spirit shines forth as the reward of all yogic disciplines.

The liberating knowledge being there, the mind can bind the Spirit no longer. It returns to Nature, its origin. The disintegrated strands go back to Nature. The *buddhi* too, being disintegrated into its constituents, becomes merged into Nature and remains there forever. This means that the entire subtle body of the yogi merges into Nature. The physical body may continue till death and then resolves into its constituent elements. Thus the yogi attains final liberation which is complete aloofness or isolation of Spirit from Nature. Here the reverse of evolution reaches its last stage. Starting the practice of concentration on the gross physical objects, the yogi succeeds in fixing the mind on finer and finer entities. The finest of all is Nature, their origin. The Spirit being liberated from the bondage of the strands, shines forth in its pure intelligence. The *Yoga-sūtras* conclude saying:

> Since the gunas no longer have any purpose to serve for the purusha, they resolve themselves into Prakrti. This is liberation. The purusha shines forth in its own pristine nature, as pure consciousness (YS IV.34).

There is no bliss or happiness in Yoga's concept of liberation, for all feelings belong to Nature. It is thus a state of pure consciousness. This is the end of a yogi's journey.

---

[62] Cf. Swami Prabhavananda on *Yoga-sūtra* II.27. It is to be noted that his interpretation of the seven stages is based on Advaita philosophy.

Chapter IV

THE EFFECT OF MEDITATION

A. Introduction

Having evaluated the techniques of meditation as interpreted by Swami Prabhavananda, in the present chapter we proceed to determine the effect of meditation. According to Advaita, liberation consists in knowledge, the individual self's true knowledge of itself. No work can effect liberation. Meditation, if it is regarded as a work, is of no avail in the pursuit of liberation. In this chapter we propose to specify the role of meditation in effecting final liberation. With this in mind we shall discuss the 'relationship' between the individual self and the Absolute; bondage of the individual self; the theory of liberation; and meditation as a final step towards the liberating knowledge.

B. The absolute and the individual self

The supreme goal of man is the identification of the individual self with the Absolute, according to Advaita. The Absolute is Brahman or Self according to the difference of approach from the objective or subjective point of view. Brahman and Self caught the attention of the Upaniṣadic seers. Earlier we have seen how Swami Prabhavananda interprets the two fundamental ideas of the Upaniṣads.[1] We have also followed the discussion of Brahman in the Upaniṣads in connection with the forms of meditation.[2] Here we shall consider it only under a single perspective: the Absolute as 'related to' man.

---

[1] See p. 2, above.

[2] See chapter two, pp. 31-38.

1. *The Absolute in Advaita*

The Upaniṣads teach that Brahman, the ultimate ground of the universe, is same as the Self in man. From the large number of passages which give expression to this thought we have to select only a few of the more relevant ones. The Bṛhad-āraṇyaka Upaniṣad 2.4 discloses penetrating insight into the nature of the Self. The teaching begins with the sentence: "not for love of the husband is a husband dear, but for love of the Soul (Ātman) a husband is dear" (BU 2.4.5). Similarly, all objects of the world, such as a wife, sons, wealth, Brahminhood, Kṣatriyahood, worlds, gods, beings, etc., are dear not for their own sake, but for the sake of the Self. The immediate conclusion of this verse is: "It is the Soul (Ātman) that should be seen, that should be hearkened to, that should be thought on, that should be pondered on" (v. 5). This means that the knowledge of the Self is the highest of all knowledge; not to know It is to be ignored by all (v. 6). This is expressed by a number of images: when a drum is beaten (v. 7), a conch blown (v. 8), a lute played (v. 9), one is not able to grasp the external sounds, but by grasping the instruments the sounds are grasped at the same time. As from a fire burning with damp fuel various smokes go forth, so from the eternal Brahman are breathed out all knowledge and all wisdom (v. 10). The Self is the point of union for all beings, as the ocean for all waters, skin for all kinds of touch, nostrils for all smells, tongue for all tastes, ear for all sounds, etc. (v. 11). But it can be objected that if the Self is the only Reality, why does It hide Itself? Yājñavalkya employs another image in answer to this question: As a lump of salt dropped into water becomes dissolved in water and cannot be taken out again, but it tastes salt, so is the Self (v. 12). The Chāndogya Upaniṣad 6.1 uses a series of images to mean that all learning is useless unless one knows the truth with regard to the Self. The instruction about the Self is the basis of all knowledge (v. 3). As by knowing a lump of clay all that is made of clay is known (v. 4), by knowing a copper ornament all things made of copper are known (v. 5), by knowing a pair of nail-scissors all that is made of iron is known (v. 6), so is the knowledge of the Self, knowing which all is known. Other Upaniṣads too support this view: "Lo, verily, with the seeing of, with the harkening to, with the thinking of, and with the understanding of the Soul, this world-all is known" (BU 2.4.5). The Muṇḍaka Upaniṣad 1.1.3 reports how

Śaunaka approached Aṅgiras, asking 'Through understanding of what does all this world become understood?'

Having established the doctrine of the sole reality of Brahman (CU 3.14.1; Mā U 2) and the unreality of all else (CU 6.4.1ff; Mā U 7), the Upaniṣads refer to Brahman and Self as synonymous (BU 4.4.5; Mā U 2). The first principle of the universe dwells within man as the subject within:

> He who, dwelling in the earth, yet is other than the earth, whom the earth does not know, whose body the earth is, who controls the earth from within — He is your Soul, the Inner Controller, the Immortal (BU 3.7.3).

The Self, this passage teaches, is the 'inner controller' in everything. The same Upaniṣad continues:

> He who, dwelling in the semen, yet is other than the semen, whom the semen does not know, whose body the semen is, who controls the semen from within — He is your Soul, the Inner Controller, the Immortal (BU 3.7.23).

The Kaṭha Upaniṣad speaks of the eternal Person as abiding in one's self:

> A Person of the measure of a thumb
> Stands in the midst of one's self (*ātman*),
> Lord of what has been and of what is to be,
> One does not shrink away from Him (KU 4.12).

The equation of the 'self' of the universe with the 'self' of man is expressed by "that thou art" (CU 6.8.7) and "I am Brahman" (BU 1.4.10). Swami Prabhavananda considers it a startling discovery and the climax of experience. As he puts it:

> Endless change without, and at the heart of the change an abiding reality — Brahman. Endless change within, and at the heart of the change an abiding reality — Ātman. Were there then two realities? No, answered the ṛṣis, Brahman and Ātman are one and the same. And they summed up, the prodigious affirmation in the words Tat Tvam asi — That thou art.[3]

This knowledge of the identity of the Supreme Self and the individual self is the source of all peace and bliss. The supreme bliss is to be sought in the realization of this identity, says one Upaniṣad:

---

[3] SWAMI PRABHAVANANDA, SHI, p. 55.

'This is it!' — thus they recognize
The highest, indescribable happiness.
How, now, shall I understand 'this'?
Does it shine [of itself] or does it shine in reflection?

The sun shines not there, nor the moon and stars,
These lightnings shine not, much less this (earthly) fire!
After Him, as He shines, doth everything shine,
This whole world is illumined with His light (KU 5.14-15).

In order to see the nature of this identity we have to clarify another concept, namely the individual self.

2. *The Individual self in Advaita*

In his *Vedic Religion and Philosophy* Swami Prabhavananda examines, with remarkable insight, the nature and status of the individual self or embodied self (*jīva*) in Advaita.[4] Man is called *jīva,* that is he who breathes, denoting his biological and physiological nature. The Kaṭha Upaniṣad 3.4 describes the individual self as the enjoyer (*bhoktar*), the self united with body, senses and mind. This description further appears in the Śvetāśvatara Upaniṣad 1.8-9 (*bhoktṛ*), I.12 and 5.7 (*bhoktā*). Again, he is the doer (*kartṛ*) or the agent of actions (Praśna U 4.5).

In order to explain the nature of the individual self Swami Prabhavananda refers to a story told in the Muṇḍaka Upaniṣad 3.1.1. It is a story of two birds sitting on the branches of a tree. The birds referred to are the individual self and the Supreme Self.[5]

Two birds, fast bound companions,
Clasp close the self-same tree.
Of these two, the one eats sweet fruit;
The other looks on without eating (MU 3.1.1).

Concluding his interpretation of this passage, Swami Prabhavananda says:

> Though living on the self-same tree, the Individual self, deluded by the forgetfulness of its divine nature, grieves, bewildered by its own helplessness. And when the same one recognizes the worshipful Lord as its own true Self, and beholds His glory, it becomes free from all grief. Thus, when the individual realizes the self-luminous Lord, the cause

[4] Id., *Vedic Religion and Philosophy,* pp. 52-74.

[5] This story is retold in SU 4.6. But it seems to be an adaptation of RV i.164.20. Compare also KU 3.1.

of all causes, it sheds all impurities and realizes its identity with the Universal Self.[6]

It is to be remarked that in the Muṇḍaka Upaniṣad 3.1.1 and its sequels, what is implied is the contrast between individual self and the Supreme Self, rather than their unity. But in the Bṛhad-āraṇyaka and Chāndogya Upaniṣads the view maintained is that they are essentially one. We quote here BU 4.5.15:

> For where there is duality, as it were, there one sees another; there one smells another; there one tastes another; there one speaks to another; there one hears another; there one understands another. But where everything has become just one's own self, then whereby and whom would one see? (BU 4.5.15).

Many passages in the Chāndogya Upaniṣad indicate that the individual self is non-different from the Universal Self. The *Śāṇḍilya vidyā* which affirms the essential oneness of the individual self and the Supreme Brahman is explained in the same Upaniṣad as follows:

> This Soul of mine within the heart is smaller than the grain of rice, or a barley-corn, or a mustard-seed, or a grain of millet, or the kernel of a grain of millet; this Soul of mine within the heart is greater than the earth, greater than the atmosphere, greater than the sky, greater than these worlds.
>
> Containing all works, containing all desires, containing all odors, containing all tastes, encompassing this whole world, the unspeaking, the unconcerned — this is the Soul of mine within the heart, this is Brahma. Into him I shall enter on departing hence (CU 3.14.3-4).

Advaita has accepted this latter view. It treats the nature of the self from two levels: transcendental and phenomenal. From the transcendental viewpoint each self is the whole indivisible Brahman, since the latter does not admit anything outside Itself. Each self is therefore non-dual, immortal, ever pure, ever free and identical (*ananya*) with Brahman. But from the phenomenal point of view Advaita admits a plurality of individual selves. Śaṁkara compares them to the images of the sun reflected in water. As the one and the same luminous sun being reflected in many water-vessels appears to be many suns, even so resplendent Brahman, though one-without-a-second, is individualized and separately abides in all the

---

[6] SWAMI PRABHAVANANDA, *Vedic Religion and Philosophy*, p. 58.

individual beings.[7] The reflection of the sun is only the sun appearing as such. It has no existence apart from the sun. Similarly, the individual selves are only Brahman appearing as such.

We have been discussing the Absolute. We have also seen the nature of the individual self, which we emphasized as the Absolute appearing as individual existence. But this truth regarding its own true nature is hidden from the self. The following section examines the implications of this ignorance on the part of the individual self.

3. *Bondage of the Individual self*

Having discussed the Absolute and Its 'relation' to the individual self, we have now to deal with an important problem which may be stated thus: if the individual self is identical with Brahman, why is it unaware of this identity? Liberation according to Advaita is the knowledge of the self's ultimate nature as Brahman. Bondage is the ignorance of the same. Therefore the idea of liberation presupposes a prior state of bondage, called in Sanskrit *saṁsāra.* Swami Prabhavananda translates it as 'empirical existence.'[8] The doctrine of *saṁsāra* is the theory that according to one's good or bad actions in this life one enters at death into the body of a higher or a lower being. The Upaniṣads already elaborate this theory:

> Accordingly, those who are of pleasant conduct here — the prospect is, indeed, that they will enter a pleasant womb, either the womb of a Brahman, or the womb of a Kshatriya, or the womb of a Vaiśya. But those who are of stinking conduct here — the prospect is, indeed, that they will enter a stinking womb, either the womb of a dog, or the womb of a swine, or the womb of an outcast (*caṇḍāla*) (CU 5.10.7).[9]

---

[7] Cf. *Śaṁkara Bhāṣya on the Vedānta Sūtras* III.ii.18.

[8] Cf. Swami Prabhavananda, SHI, p. 311.

[9] Other Upaniṣads also elaborate this doctrine. Thus:

> By the delusions (*moha*) of imagination, touch, and sight,
> And by eating, drinking, and impregnation, there is a birth and development of the self (*ātman*).
> According unto his deeds (*karman*) the embodied one successively
> Assumes forms in various conditions.
> Coarse and fine, many in number,
> The embodied one chooses forms according to his own qualities.
> [Each] subsequent cause of his union with them is seen to be
> Because of the quality of his acts and of himself
> (SU 5.11-12).

In some other passages there is mention that *saṁsāra* is the consequence not only of works but also of ignorance. Thus:

> Manifoldly living in ignorance,

The doctrine of *saṁsāra* is intimately connected with the doctrine of the Self as the eternal reality in man. While birth is the connection of the Self with the body, death indicates Its separation from the body. The repetition of the cycle of births and deaths is *saṁsāra*. According to Swami Prabhavananda the individual self, in so far as it is associated with an individual psycho-somatic mechanism, is always being born and dying again until it is finally liberated.[10]

The fifteenth chapter of the Gītā begins with a description of the Cosmic Fig-tree, a symbol of *saṁsāra*. Kṛṣṇa asks to cut it down with the stout axe of detachment (BG 15.3-4) and to take refuge in the primeval Person (BG 15.6).

Commenting on the Kaṭha Upaniṣad 5.7, Śaṁkara defends the idea of *saṁsāra* saying that otherwise the scriptural injunctions would become meaningless.[11] For according to him the scriptures conceive of liberation as coming only through perfect knowledge which is of the nature of *triputi-bheda,* the untying of the three knots of knowledge, consisting of the subject, the object and the process of knowledge. In the same text he asks: whither do the limiting adjuncts of the individual self go at death? If the doctrine of *saṁsāra* is not admitted, he believes, there should have been automatically absolute union with Brahman at the moment of death. According to Swami Prabhavananda liberation from *saṁsāra* means the absolute merging of the individual self in Brahman, dismissing the erroneous notion that it is distinct from Brahman. Therefore if we are to understand the nature of liberation we have to examine also the nature of the prior state of bondage. In this section we shall set forth the implications of bondage as taught by Advaita.

The crux of the problem consists in reconciling the ordinary experience of the universe of many objects and the metaphysical insight into Brahman, the only Reality. In other words, the ques-

---

They think to themselves, childishly: "We have accomplished our aim!"
Since doers of deeds (*karmin*) do not understand, because of passion (*rāga*),
Therefore, when their words are exhausted, they sink down wretched.
Thinking sacrifice and merit is the chiefest thing,
Naught better do they know — deluded!
Having had enjoyment on the top of the heaven won by good works,
They re-enter this world, or a lower (MU 1.2.9-10).

Some go into a womb
For the embodiment of a corporeal being.
Others go into a stationary thing
According to their deeds (*karman*), according to their knowledge (KU 5.7).

10 Cf. Swami Prabhavananda on *Yoga-sūtra* II.9.

11 Cf. *Śaṁkara Bhāṣya on Vedānta Sūtras* IV.ii.8.

tion how does Brahman become the individual self, the Infinite finite, has to be answered. To solve the dilemma Advaita offers the doctrine of *māyā*. Hence it becomes necessary to speak of *māyā*. However we do not intend to treat all the aspects of *māyā*. We shall give only the essential ones relating to the concealment of true knowledge on the part of the self.

The concept of *māyā* which occupies a pivotal position in Advaita appears even in the earliest scriptures of Hinduism, but with a different meaning. The Ṛg Veda often uses the word *māyā* to mean the supernatural powers of celestial beings, especially of Varuṇa, Mitra and Indra.

Partisans of Advaita see an amplification of this concept in the Upaniṣads. In a well-known prayer in the Bṛhad-āraṇyaka Upaniṣad the devotee begs:

> From the unreal (*asat*) lead me to the real (*sat*)!
> From darkness lead me to light!
> From death lead me to immortality! (BU 1.3.28).

In this they identify unreality, darkness and death with *māyā*. The same Upaniṣad, in a prayer by a dying person, states that the face of truth is covered by a golden disc (BU 5.15.1). This prayer is found in the Īśa Upaniṣad as a prayer for the vision of truth (Īśa U 15). "With a golden vessel is the face of the real covered" (Maitrī U 6.35) is perhaps another version of the same prayer. Advaitins hold that the "golden disc" that veils reality is *māyā*. Even in the teachings of Yājñavalkya on the sole reality of the Self and the unreality of all else apart from It, they claim a reference to *māyā*. It may be admitted that in the Upaniṣads there is the germ of the *māyā* doctrine, later to be developed by Gauḍapāda and Śaṁkara as the cardinal point of Advaita.[12] Swami Prabhavananda believes that in accepting *māyā* as the theory of the universe, Śaṁkara is solving the most difficult of all philosophical problems: the relation between Brahman and the universe.[13] Brahman is not transformed into the universe, but simply appears as the universe to us who are under the power of *māyā*.

---

[12] A scholar like George Thibaut in *The Vedanta Sutras of Bādarāyana* (New York, 1962), p. cxvii n. 1 observes: "It is well known that, with the exception of the Svetâsvatara and Maitrâyanîya, none of the chief Upanishads exhibits the word 'mâyâ'. The term indeed occurs in one place in the Brihadâranyaka; but that passage is a quotation from the Rik Samhitâ in which mâyâ means 'creative power'."

[13] Cf. Swami Prabhavananda, SHI, p. 284.

Māyā has two modes: cosmic (*samaṣti*) and individual (*vyaṣti*). In this section, which deals with the bondage of the individual self, we are more concerned with the subjective aspect of *māyā* known as ignorance. For, it seems that Swami Prabhavananda lays more stress on this, which, he says, "bars the way to liberation." [14]

The Upaniṣads describe ignorance as the source of delusion. It is 'seeking the stable among things which are unstable here' (KU 4.2). In another place there is a description of people living in the midst of ignorance, going about like blind men led by the blind (KU 2.5). According to the Chāndogya Upaniṣad ignorance is a 'false covering' (CU 8.3.1-2).

Swami Prabhavananda defines ignorance as "that which causes us to move farther away from the Self and obscures our knowledge of the Truth." [15] This definition shows that although ignorance seems to be negative, a mere absence of knowledge, it is a positive entity. To consider it negatively does not do justice to the idea. Ignorance has an empirical reality, although the nature of this reality is styled as indescribable (*anirvacanīya*), as it is neither real nor unreal nor real-unreal.[16]

Śaṁkara begins his commentary on the *Vedānta Sūtras* with the theory of superimposition (*adhyāsa*). Having stated that two things entirely opposed to each other as darkness and light cannot be identified, he says:

> Hence it follows that it is wrong to superimpose upon the subject — whose Self is intelligence, and which has for its sphere the notion of the Ego — the object whose sphere is the notion of the Non-Ego, and the attributes of the object, and vice versâ to superimpose the subject and the attributes of the subject on the object. In spite of this it is on the part of man a natural procedure — which has its cause in wrong knowledge — not to distinguish the two entities (object and subject) and their respective attributes, although they are absolutely distinct,

---

14 *Ibid.*, p. 205.

15 *Ibid.*, p. 292.

16 Krishna Warrier, *Concept of Mukti in Advaita Vedānta* (Madras, 1961), pp. 322-323, describes the special nature of ignorance as follows: "... *avidyā* is a category *sui generis,* not real enough to set itself up as a rival to Brahman, and yet not unreal like the hare's horn. In short, whereas Brahman is a transcendental and eternal reality, *avidyā* is an empirical fact. The man in the street considers the world of *avidyā* as real. One who is learned in the *śāstras,* viz. the man of the spiritual insight, regards it as unreal or *tuccha* while the metaphysician, intellectually, accounts it neither real nor unreal."

> but to superimpose upon each the characteristic nature and the attributes of the other, and thus, coupling the Real and the Unreal ...[17]

This superimposition which Śaṁkara identifies as ignorance, gives rise to a radical confusion.[18] It is not a mere intellectual error; it affects the whole man. This is exemplified in the imagery of a rope, seen in twilight by a man, and thought to be a snake; and mother-of-pearl appearing silver. In *Aparokṣānubhūti*, a small work attributed to Śaṁkara, many illustrations are used to explain the nature of superimposition.[19] To see the universe apart from Brahman is like seeing blueness in the sky; water in the mirage; and the human figure in a stump of a tree; it is purely illusory, like the appearance of a ghost in an empty place, a castle in the air, or a second moon in the sky. The author goes on to affirm that just as it is water that appears as ripples and waves in the ocean, or it is copper that appears as different vessels, or it is earth that appears in the form of jar and threads as cloth, so it is Brahman that appears under the name of the universe. These are but popular expressions of the theory of superimposition. But the impact of superimposition is not fully manifest there. Because, there could be an excuse for such confusions, when there exist some similarities between the real and the apparent. The nature of ignorance is fully manifest when one perceives only the universe in place of Brahman.[20]

Hence according to Advaita the causes of the superimposition, e. g., a snake for a rope, are the sense contact with the rope, impressions of previous knowledge of a snake in the mind, and the defects of the sense organs. When the defective sense organs come into contact with rope, there takes place a mental modification which

---

[17] *Śaṁkara Bhāṣya on Vedānta Sūtras* 1.i. Quotations from the *Vedānta Sūtras* are taken from *The Vedanta Sūtras of Bādarāyana with the commentary by Śaṅkara,* trans. George Thibaut (Dover Publications, New York, 1962).

[18] Learned people consider superimposition to be *avidyā.* Cf. *ibid.*

[19] Cf. *Aparokṣānubhūti,* work attributed to Śrī Śaṁkara. Text with word-for-word Translation and Notes. Trans. Swami Vimuktananda (Advaita Ashrama, Calcutta, 1973), vv. 61-64.

[20] The process of superimposition is explained by Śaṁkara as folows: "Adhyâsa takes place when the idea of one of two things not being dismissed from the mind, the idea of the second thing is superimposed on that of the first thing; so that together with the superimposed idea the former idea remains attached to the thing on which the second idea is superimposed. When e. g. the idea of (the entity) Brahman superimposes itself upon the idea of the name, the latter idea continues in the mind and is not driven out by the former." *Śaṁkara Bhāṣya on Vedānta Sūtras* III.iii.9.

does not correspond to the reality outside. As a result, the ignorance in the person, coinciding with the prior knowledge of snake, creates the perception of the rope-snake.

Now we are in a better position to understand the full significance of the individual self's bondage.[21] Ignorance makes it subject to limitations of the body; led by passions, feeling of attachment to pleasurable things and aversion for painful things, it is bound to the wheel of birth and death for the enjoyment of its desired objects. Śaṁkara explains how the non-enlightened individual self is unable to eliminate ignorance and recognize itself to be Brahman:

> Before the rise of discriminative knowledge the nature of the individual soul, which is (in reality) pure light, is non-discriminated as it were from its limiting adjuncts consisting of body, senses, mind, sense-objects and feelings, and appears as consisting of the energies of seeing and so on.[22]

In conclusion we may add Swami Prabhavananda's remark that spiritual freedom consists in the cessation of this ignorance regarding the individual self.[23] Ignorance is without beginning but removable by knowledge. According to the Śvetāśvatara Upaniṣad "ignorance is a thing perishable" (SU 5.1). "Individual ignorance is beginningless, but it can end at any moment; it is lost when a man achieves spiritual illumination." [24]

How this final release is effected makes the subject-matter of the following section.

C. Liberation

The theory of liberation (*mukti*) underwent many modifications before it reached its ultimate non-dualistic form in Advaita. In the

---

[21] A text in the Maitrī Upaniṣad describes the individual self's bondage as follows:

> This [elemental soul], verily, is overcome by Nature's (*prakṛti*) qualities (*guṇa*). Now, because of being overcome he goes on to confusedness; because of confusedness, he sees not the blessed Lord (*prabhu*), the causer of action, who stands within oneself (*ātma-stha*). Borne along and defiled by the stream of Qualities (*guṇa*), unsteady, wavering, bewildered, full of desire, distracted, this one goes on to the state of self-conceit (*abhimānatva*). In thinking 'This is I' and 'That is mine,' he binds himself with his self, as does a bird with a snare (Maitrī U 3.2).

[22] *Śaṁkara Bhāṣya on Vedānta Sūtras* I.iii.19.

[23] Cf. Swami Prabhavananda, SHI, p. 292.

[24] *Ibid.*, p. 288.

Upaniṣads when Brahman was recognized as the one Reality, unity with It meant liberation. When finally Brahman and the Self were identified, unity of the individual self with Brahman was considered to be the highest ideal.

The Upaniṣads employ various similes to describe the nature of liberation. The Chāndogya Upaniṣad compares it to a horse's shaking off its hairs and the moon freeing itself from eclipse (CU 8. 13.1). The similes of a blind man gaining sight and a sick man getting cured are applied to it (CU 8.4.2). The Muṇḍaka Upaniṣad has another beautiful image:

> As the flowing rivers in the ocean
> Disappear, quitting name and form,
> So the knower, being liberated from name and form,
> Goes unto the Heavenly Person, higher than the high (MU 3.2.8).

Swami Prabhavananda holds that liberation is a state of oneness with Brahman. It is the self-extinction in Brahman (*Brahma-nirvāṇa*), the "extinction of ego, the false self, in the higher Self — the source of all knowledge, of all existence, and of all happiness."[25] The individual self in reality is Brahman. It is only ignorance that hides this truth. This is the self's bondage. Liberation is the cessation of the same.[26] Thus we see that Swami Prabhavananda's view of liberation is essentially Advaitic.

Liberation is not a state newly attained, but belongs to the very nature of the self. It is "the birthright of every man."[27] It cannot be regarded as a becoming something which previously did not exist. It is no becoming but a being. For reason tells us that had it been a becoming, it could not be the ultimate ideal. Everything

---

[25] *Ibid.,* p. 110.

[26] The Maitrī Upaniṣad has the following description:

Hence a person who has the marks of determination, conception, and self-conceit is bound. Hence, in being the opposite of that, he is liberated. Therefore one should stand free from determination, free from conception, free from self-conceit. This is the mark of liberation (*mokṣa*). This is the pathway to Brahma here in this world. This is the opening of the door here in this world. By it one will go to the farther shore of this darkness, for therein all desires are contained. On this point they quote:

> When cease the five
> [Sense-] knowledges, together with the mind,
> And the intellect stirs not —
> That, they say, is the highest course (Maitrī U 6.30).

[27] Swami Prabhavananda, *Vedic Religion and Philosophy,* pp. 81-82.

that comes to be is transient; the same may also return to nothingness. Therefore liberation is not properly a new beginning; it is the realization of that which exists from eternity but has hitherto been concealed like a hidden treasure (CU 8.3.2). It means, not a becoming something that had no previous existence, but only becoming aware of something so far hidden. The knowledge "I am Brahman" removes the veil of untruth. In other words liberation is the "coming into its own of the divine Self, and this Self is beyond time, which, with space and a thousand other conditions of human life, belongs only to the finite world." [28]

In the light of this explanation of liberation we can better understand the way it is effected. If the individual self in its real nature is Brahman, and if it is only due to ignorance that it appears finite, bound and miserable, then with the elimination of ignorance should come simultaneously its liberation.

In numerous texts the Upaniṣads teach that he who knows Brahman is liberated. The Kaṭha Upaniṣad connects liberation with knowledge:

> Higher than the Unmanifest, however, is the Person (Purusha),
> All-pervading and without any mark (*a-liṅga*) whatever.
> Knowing which, a man is liberated
> And goes to immortality.
>
> His form (*rūpa*) is not to be beheld.
> No one soever sees Him with the eye.
> He is framed by the heart, by the thought, by the mind.
> They who know That become immortal (KU 6.8-9).

The Upaniṣads say that the knower of Brahman becomes Brahman (MU 3.2.9). Even gods cannot prevent his becoming thus (BU 1.4.10). No wealth on earth is comparable to the knowledge of Brahman. His greatness is eternal (BU 4.4.23). The Upaniṣad indeed says:

> Truly, it is Life (*prāṇa*) that shines forth in all things!
> Understanding this, one becomes a knower. There is no superior speaker.
> Having delight in the Soul (Ātman), having pleasure in the Soul, doing the rites,
> Such a one is the best of Brahma-knowers (MU 3.1.4).

---

[28] Id., SHI, p. 62.

We propose in the first place to use these passages to throw light upon the teaching of Swami Prabhavananda on the Advaita concept of liberation. He says:

> The illumined seer does not merely know Brahman, he is Brahman, he is Existence, he is Knowledge. Absolute freedom is not something to be attained, absolute knowledge is not something to be won, Brahman is not something to be found anew. It is only māyā which has to be pierced, ignorance which has to be overcome. The process of discrimination is a negative process. The positive fact, our real nature, eternally exists. We are Brahman — and only ignorance drives us from knowledge of the fact.[29]

From this text it is clear that for Swami Prabhavananda knowledge of Brahman is itself liberation. Nor is this knowledge a means to liberation. He who has realized 'I am Brahman' has already achieved the highest goal of life. Having gained this knowledge, the Brahmanas became disgusted with learning (BU 3.5.1); because the ancients knew this they did not desire offspring, saying "what shall we do with offspring, we whose is this Soul, this world?" (BU 4.4.22) and became mendicants.

For this reason it is a special kind of knowledge. The one who gains intuition of the Brahman-Self equation unites oneself in consciousness to Brahman. Swami Prabhavananda calls this consciousness 'transcendental consciousness.'[30] It is a superconscious state in which man experiences his identity with Brahman. He becomes completely absorbed in Brahman, like salt dissolved in water so there is absolutely no sense of ego at all. This is the threshold of spiritual experience according to Advaita.[31]

With the dawn of transcendental consciousness the individual self definitely recognizes its identity with Brahman. This ineffable experience is enough to remove every trace of body-consciousness. But not all seekers leave the body at the first instant; some retain

---

[29] *Ibid.*, p. 295.

[30] Cf. *ibid.*, p. 260.

[31] Swami Prabhavananda describes the experience in transcendental consciousness as follows: "In samadhi the experience is not of many ideas or many truths, but rather the *one* truth of God. In the lower form of samadhi, the idea of ego, separate from God, is there, but only in relation to and in connection with God. The universe of many is then obliterated. But after one returns from samadhi, he does not find himself as ignorant as before, but he finds that "he lives, moves, and has his being in God." SWAMI PRABHAVANANDA, "Samadhi or Transcendental Consciousness," in: *Vedanta for the Western World*, p. 221.

the body. This concept is called liberation-in-life and forms one of the most characteristic features of Advaita.

1. *Liberation-in-Life* (*Jīvan-mukti*)

In conformity with the Advaita theory of liberation Swami Prabhavananda says that liberation may be attained either during the course of one's life or at the moment of death.[32] The one who has achieved liberation during life is called 'the living-free' (*jīvan-mukta*). But the concept of liberation during life is not an invention of Advaita; we find evidence for it in the early religious literature of India. The Kaṭha Upaniṣad 5.1, in the following statement:

> By ruling over the eleven-gated citadel
> Of the Unborn, the Un-crooked-minded one,
> One sorrows not.
> But when liberated [from the body], he is liberated indeed,

teaches that there are two stages of liberation: that which begins here and that which leads after death to final liberation. The mortal becomes immortal even here (KU 6.14,15). This hints at the doctrine of liberation from the bonds of empirical existence. Even more expressive is the Bṛhad-āraṇyaka Upaniṣad:

> When are liberated all
> The desires that lodge in one's heart,
> Then a mortal becomes immortal!
> Therein he reaches Brahma (BU 4.4.7).

Swami Prabhavananda speaks in many places of liberation-in-life as the supreme ideal for man. Translating BG 2.54-72, he calls the living-free, a seer and enlightened.[33] Whatever he may do or howsoever he may act, he is free from craving and is forever established in the knowledge of Brahman. Although he perceives the universe, still it is not real to him. Always and everywhere he is conscious only of Brahman. For the Upaniṣad says: "Where one sees nothing else, hears nothing else, understands nothing else — that is a Plenum" (CU 7.24.1). His vision of the world changes in the sense that he immediately realizes the world's truth as Brahman. Everything in the world reveals to him its essential nature as Brahman.

---

[32] Cf. SWAMI PRABHAVANANDA, SHI, p. 62.
[33] Cf. ID., *Song of God*, pp. 93ff.

In this way he verifies the Upaniṣadic dictum that everything is enveloped by God (Īśa U 1).

There seems little difference between the external actions of the living-free and those of ordinary people. Swami Prabhavananda says that the living-free, although he continues to live and act, is not bound by *karma*.[34] In fact here he uses *karma* in a different sense and understands by it only such actions which are motivated by egoism. The actions of the living-free are in this sense no actions at all since they are not led by the ego. But this does not mean that the enlightened take refuge in a false quietism. On the contrary, they work for the welfare of humanity (BG 12.13). They are neither vain nor anxious about the result of their works (BG 12.16). That is why Swami Prabhavananda says: "he lives only to exhaust what are known as the prārabdha karmas." [35]

We shall end this description of the living-free and say that in Advaita the highest aim of human endeavour is the realization of Brahman. Some gain this intuitive realization during life while others only at death.

2. *Liberation-at-Death* (*Videha-mukti*)

While *jīvan-mukti* is deliverance during life, *videha-mukti* is deliverance at the moment of death. Swami Prabhavananda says:

> For him who has not achieved mokṣa during life there is the possibility of obtaining it at death — provided that during his life he has disciplined and prepared himself for it making it his sole aim.[36]

It is the final deliverance of the self from all the traits of worldly existence. The Kaṭha Upaniṣad employs the image of water pouring into water,

> As pure water poured forth into pure
> Becomes the very same,
> So becomes the soul (*ātman*), O Gautama,
> Of the seer (*muni*) who has understanding (KU 4.15),

from which Advaitins conclude the metaphysical identity between the individual self and the Supreme Self. In liberation at death

[34] Cf. Id., SHI, p. 112. See chapter one n. 22, above.

[35] *Ibid. Prārabdha karma* is the portion of the stored-up *karma* from past lives which has begun to bear fruit in the present life, in which it must be exhausted.

[36] Swami Prabhavananda, SHI, p. 62.

this truth of non-separation shines simultaneously with the fall of the body and final release takes place at that very moment.

Two other types of liberation are immediate liberation (*sādyo-mukti*) and gradual liberation (*krama-mukti*). We just mention them for the sake of completeness and pass on since Swami Prabhavananda has not discussed them. Immediate liberation is logically identical with liberation at death since there is no time needed between the dawn of the saving knowledge and liberation itself. When the deliverance is only partial and temporary owing to the aspirant's failure to obtain the saving knowledge, they are obliged to descend to Brahman's world by the way of the gods (*devayāna*). During their sojourn in the world of Brahman these semi-liberated souls develop their fitness for final liberation which they gain at the time of the world's dissolution.[37]

In this section we have been developing the Advaitic doctrine of liberation and we found that it is the same as knowledge of the Self. We now try to answer the question: how does this saving knowledge come? Our point is that meditation effects this knowledge of the Self. The spiritual experience in the meditation on the great saying of "That thou art" is hoped to form a particular feature of the following article.

D. Way to liberation: Meditation on the great saying (mahā-vākya)

Above, we have made it clear that the Advaita idea of liberation is the realization of the individual self's identity with Brahman, arising from the knowledge of Brahman. Even so, there is a problem. The Upaniṣads seem to emphasize the difficulty of knowing Brahman. We cite here a few texts:

> There the eye goes not;
> Speech goes not, nor the mind.
> We know not, we understand not
> How one would teach It.
> Other, indeed, is It than the known,
> And moreover above the unknown.
> — Thus have we heard of the ancients (*pūrva*)
> Who to us have explained It (Kena U 3).

[37] Cf. *Śaṁkara Bhāṣya on Vedānta Sūtras* IV.iii.10.

Brahman transcends the ordinary means of knowledge:

> Not by speech, not by mind,
> Not by sight can He be apprehended.
> How can He be comprehended
> Otherwise than by one's saying 'He is'? (KU 6.12)

In the Bṛhad-āraṇyaka Upaniṣad we have some mystical descriptions of Brahman:

> You could not see the seer of seeing. You could not hear the hearer of hearing. You could not think the thinker of thinking. You could not understand the understander of understanding (BU 3.4.2).
>
> Verily, O Gārgī, that Imperishable is the unseen Seer, the unheard Hearer, the unthought Thinker, the ununderstood Understander (BU 3.8.11).
>
> ... But where everything has become just one's own self, then whereby and whom would one see? then whereby and whom would one smell? then whereby and whom would one taste? then whereby and to whom would one speak? then whereby and whom would one hear? then whereby and of whom would one think? then whereby and whom would one touch? then whereby and whom would one understand? whereby would one understand him by means of whom one understands this All? (BU 4.5.15)

The Upaniṣadic statements quoted above declare that the Absolute is beyond the ordinary understanding of man. It is different from the known and the unknown, but It is not unknowable. The Upaniṣads allude to tradition (Kena U 3). The ancients had discovered some kind of method to see the 'Seer of seeing.' What would be that method?

In order to rediscover that method Swami Prabhavananda retells a story recorded in the Chāndogya Upaniṣad[38] It is a conversation between a father and a son. This Upaniṣad repeats the phrase "That thou art" as a refrain nine times in the sixth chapter alone. Advaitins hold that the phrase indicates the ultimate oneness of the individual self with Brahman.[39] This truth is expressed in three words: *tat*

---

[38] Cf. SWAMI PRABHAVANANDA, SHI, pp. 55-58. The reference is to CU 6.11-15.

[39] "*Tat tvam asi*" has been variously interpreted by the different schools of Vedānta to fit their teaching. For Rāmānuja, the Viśiṣṭādvaitin, it means that God is the self of the individual self. Mādhva, the Dvaitin, reads the text as 'atat tvam asi' (thou art not that) and argues that it establishes the difference between the individual self and the Universal Self. Śaṁkara interprets it in the sense that the

tvam asi.[40] In order to better understand it, we shall proceed to give an exegesis of the Chāndogya Upaniṣad chapter 6, one of the most important portions of the Upaniṣad. The chapter is divided into 16 sections.

Section 1. Introduction

2-3. Uddālaka explains how the One Existent enters into the three primordial elements, namely, heat, water and food and puts forth the living self.

4. Teaching of the threefold development. All things proceed from the three primordial elements.

5-6. Illustrations of the threefold nature.

7. The importance of physical needs.

It is in section 8 that the famous text *tat tvam asi* appears for the first time. "That is the Reality (*satya*). That is Ātman (Soul). That thou art, Śvetaketu." The text is repeated at the end of sections from 8-16.

8. On the conditions of
   (a) sleep
   (b) hunger
   (c) thirst
   (d) death

From sections 9-16 Uddālaka employs different illustrations to teach the indwelling Spirit.

9. The illustration of honey. When bees prepare honey, they gather the juices from different trees and unite them into one. As later it cannot be distinguished from which tree a particular portion of the honey is, so also all beings reach the Being without knowing that they have reached the Being.

10. The illustration of rivers. The rivers flow eastward and westward, all entering into the sea. They go from sea to sea, the clouds lifting up the water from the sea and sending it back as rain to the sea. As these rivers, when they are united with the sea, do not know whether they are this or that river, likewise all the beings know not from whence they came.

11. The illustration of tree. If someone were to cut a great

---

individual self is not an emanation, not a part of Brahman, but fully and completely Brahman.

40 Swami Prabhavananda considers the 18 chapters of the Bhagavad-Gītā an exposition of *tat tvam asi.* Cf. SWAMI PRABHAVANANDA, SHI, p. 99.

tree at the root, it would bleed, but live; if he were to cut it at the stem, it would bleed, but live; if he were to cut at the top, it would bleed, but live. If the living self were to leave the tree, the whole tree would wither. Likewise the body dies when the living Self departs from it; but the living Self does not die.

12. The illustration of seed. In the subtle essence of seed, not visible, is the whole of the Nyagrodha tree. So also the world which has name and form has its subtle essence in the Pure Being which does not possess name and form.

13. The illustration of salt and water. Just as a piece of salt is melted in water and cannot be found, but the water tastes salt, even so Brahman is there though we do not see It in the body.

14. The illustration of a man with eyes bound. As a man blindfolded, and led away, and left in a strange place, but finally arrives home, i. e. Brahman, so also is a man who meets with a person who knows the Self, obtaining true knowledge.

15. The illustration of a sick man. When a man is gravely ill, his relatives gather around him and ask, 'Do you know me?' So long as his speech is not merged in his mind, his mind in his vital breath, his breath in his vital heat, his vital heat in the Supreme Being, he knows them. But once these are merged in the Supreme Being, he does not know them any longer.

16. The illustration of a thief bound. A man suspected of stealing is put to an ordeal. Just as the guilty man is burnt and killed by grasping the heated axe while the innocent man is not affected by grasping it, so also from untruth come bonds and from truth comes freedom.

Conclusion: CU 6.16.3: "... this whole world has that truth as its soul. That is Reality. That is Ātman (Soul). That art thou, Śvetaketu! Then he understood it from him — yea, he understood."

From this exegesis we gather three main points:

1. Uddālaka is imparting a knowledge which is of supreme importance. It is that instruction by which "what has not been heard becomes heard of, what has not been thought of becomes thought of, what has not been understood becomes understood" (CU 6.1.3).

2. This is a knowledge regarding the unity of the Self. Just as by knowing a lump of clay there are known all things made of clay (CU 6.1.4), its modifications such as jars, pots, dishes, and so on being but nominal changes, so also through knowing the Self, which

is the foundation of all individual existences (CU 6.8.7), everything is known.

3. This knowledge, which is expressed in "That is Reality. That is Ātman. That thou art, Śvetaketu," and oft repeated in Chapter 6, is the direct approach to Brahman.

With these preliminary notions we shall now try to analyse the text of the great saying.

If we are to understand the meaning of a sentence, it is essential that we know the meaning of the words of the sentence. Advaita teaches that the words 'That' and 'thou' have two meanings, one direct and another implied. Advaitins employ the illustration of a red-hot iron ball. When such a ball is said to burn something, the direct meaning of the word 'ball' is iron with the qualities of fire. In fact, it is fire that burns and not the iron ball. Hence the implied meaning of the word is fire. In a number of ślokas the teacher in *Vakyavritti* explains the direct meaning of the word 'That.'[41] Accordingly 'That' conveys the idea of Īśvara, who is Brahman associated with *māyā.* In other words, the direct meaning of 'That' is, like the red-hot iron ball, Brahman, with attributes. But Brahman, the Absolute unassociated with *māyā,* is its implied meaning.

The word 'thou' also has two meanings, direct and implied.[42] The direct meaning of it is Brahman associated with individual ignorance. That is to say, directly it conveys the idea of an individual self. But Brahman, unassociated with individual ignorance, is the implied meaning of the word 'thou.'

The third word 'art' in "That thou art" conveys the meaning of the identity of 'That' and 'thou.' But here we have to confront a problem: there seems an apparent contradiction between 'That' and 'thou.' Then how can they be said to be identical?

Advaitins have found out a way to solve the problem. For them the identity of 'That' and 'thou' is a fact established by immediate experience of the seers. Therefore, "When the direct meaning of a word in a statement does not agree with actual experience, one interprets it in terms of its implied meaning."[43] They reason that the contrasting attributes of Īśvara and the individual self are not real. It is through *māyā* that Brahman appears to have

---

[41] Cf. *Vakyavritti and Ātmajñānopadeśavidhi,* works attributed to Śrī Śaṁkara, E. T. with explanatory Notes. Trans. Swami Jagadananda (Madras, 1967), śloka 28-36.

[42] Cf. *ibid.,* śloka 11-27.

[43] *Ātmabodha,* p. 117. See also *Vakyavritti,* śloka 47.

become Īśvara; it is through ignorance the same Brahman appears to have become an individual self. These superimpositions are illusory; only Brahman, the foundation both of Īśvara and the individual self, is real and absolutely the same. This is analogous to the understanding of the proposition: 'this is that Devadatta.'[44] The attributes of Devadatta, namely, the person as existing in the past and in the present, are conflicting and as such are dismissed. The meaning thus conveyed is the self-identity of Devadatta. Similarly, "That thou art" conveys the absolute identity in the implied meaning of 'That' and 'thou.'

The understanding of the great utterance with the help of a teacher effects liberation at once only in a very few disciples. In the case of many, in order that it may result in liberation, it has to be aided by reflection and meditation. We do not intend to treat reflection here any further. In order to realize the truth of "That thou art" and to convert it into a transcendental experience the seeker has to meditate on the Self as Brahman. Śaṁkara has prescribed the following meditation on "That thou art."

> Brahman has neither name nor form; it transcends merit and demerit; it is beyond time, space, and the objects of sense-experience. Such is Brahman, and "That art Thou". Meditate upon this truth.
> It is supreme. It is beyond the expression of speech; but it is known by the eye of pure illumination. It is pure, absolute consciousness, the eternal reality. Such is Brahman, and "That art Thou". Meditate upon this truth.
> It is untouched by those six waves — hunger, thirst, grief, delusion, decay and death — which sweep the ocean of worldliness. He who seeks union with it must meditate upon it within the shrine of the heart. It is beyond the grasp of the senses. The intellect cannot understand it. It is out of the reach of thought. Such is Brahman, and "That art Thou". Meditate upon this truth.
> It is the ground upon which this manifold universe, the creation of ignorance, appears to rest. It is its own support. It is neither the gross nor the subtle universe. It is indivisible. It is beyond comparison. Such is Brahman, and "That art Thou". Meditate upon this truth.
> It is free from birth, growth, change, decline, sickness and death. It is eternal. It is the cause of the evolution of the universe, its preservation and its dissolution. Such is Brahman, and "That art Thou". Meditate upon this truth.
> It is that one Reality which appears to our ignorance as a manifold universe of names and forms and changes. Like the gold of which many ornaments are made, it remains in itself unchanged. Such is Brahman, and "That art Thou". Meditate upon this truth.

[44] Cf. *Vedāntasara,* No. 151; VC, No. 248.

> There is nothing beyond it. It is greater than the greatest. It is the innermost self, the ceaseless joy within us. It is absolute existence, knowledge and bliss. It is endless, eternal. Such is Brahman, and "That art Thou". Meditate upon this truth.[45]

We have reproduced this Advaita meditation on "That thou art" despite its length as it is a typical meditation on the great saying. With the exposition of its meaning the teacher has imparted to the disciple the clue to his spiritual life. Now it is up to him to engage in the contemplation of Brahman with a single-minded devotion.

As meditation deepens the aspirant frees himself from ignorance. He gives up the desires for external objects. He is stripped of all attachments. His mind begins to dwell constantly on Brahman. This means that the truth of non-duality which was expounded by his teacher, now rises from the level of understanding to that of experience. He knows at once that the world is an illusory appearance, that Brahman is the sole reality, and that he is non-different from Brahman. According to Advaita the realization of the identity of the self with Brahman is the highest and the most fruitful of all knowledge. It means the culmination of all that man can aspire to. The result is that all his delusions, doubts, fears and sufferings are removed forever. He ceases to be a transmigratory being. He becomes liberated.

Meditation on Brahman gains in intensity when the aspirant is without the ideas of body, senses, mind and ego. Meditating on his oneness with Brahman, he arrives at a mental state which makes him feel that he is Brahman. This mental state has the power to remove his ignorance regarding Brahman. Yet even now for him Brahman is only a mental state. When meditation grows in intensity, the mental state also is removed; there remains only consciousness reflected in the mental state. This consciousness now becomes absorbed in Brahman. Advaitins use the simile of a mirror, which when removed, the reflection of an object goes back to the original. Thus the subject-object dichotomy vanishes; That and thou become one; Pure Consciousness and individual consciousness become united. The meditant becomes immersed in the limitless ocean of effulgent Bliss. It is in this sense that Swami Prabhavananda says: "Meditation is the last step on the path of realization." [46]

---

[45] VC, Nos. 254-263.

[46] Swami Prabhavananda, SHI, p. 67.

Chapter V

SWAMI PRABHAVANANDA'S UNDERSTANDING OF CHRISTIAN MEDITATION

A. Introduction

In the year 1923 Swami Prabhavananda came to the United States to work at the Ramakrishna Mission Center in San Francisco. Ever since, he has remained in the United States, giving lectures, conducting religious worships and leading group meditations. Sure enough, the participants of these services have been Christians. Taking this fact into account and in order to bring his message home to his listeners, he has resorted to the teaching of Christ. This he has done in two ways: to explain his own religion he has references to Christ and the Holy Bible; to explain the teachings of Christ he picks up similar sayings from the scriptures of his own religion. From this we conclude that in the development of his religious thought there is a mutual influence of Hindu religion and Christianity, though he perhaps was not always aware of it. In his major works there are numerous quotations from the Holy Bible and references to Christ.[1] In this chapter we shall present his views on Christian spirituality with particular reference to Christian meditation.

B. Swami Prabhavananda's experience of Christ

Swami Prabhavananda recognizes an "intimate spiritual connection" between Christ and the Ramakrishna Order.[2] For some

---

[1] The present chapter is based on the following four works of Swami Prabhavananda: 1. *The Spiritual Heritage of India;* 2. *Religion in Practice;* 3. *How to Know God: The Yoga Aphorisms of Patañjali,* 4. *The Sermon on the Mount according to Vedanta.* In these four works Swami Prabhavananda has quoted 187 verses from the Bible: 124 from Matthew, 3 from Mark, 10 from Luke, 30 from John, 13 from Paul and 7 from Psalms and Proverbs together.

[2] Swami Prabhavananda, *The Sermon on the Mount according to Vedanta* (New

time during his intense practice of meditation, Śrī Rāmakṛṣṇa became attracted to Christ.[3] In an intense meditative mood he had a vision of the Madonna and Child. Later near the Pañcavati grove at Dakṣineśwar Christ appeared to him. Thereupon he was convinced that Christ was an incarnation of God. The disciples of Śrī Rāmakṛṣṇa, in their turn, honour Christ and quote His words to explain spiritual truths. They even see an essential unity between His message and that of the Hindu sages.

Swami Prabhavananda has written a commentary on the Sermon on the Mount, which he says represents the essence of Christ's teaching.[4] He says that he has studied the New Testament in the same way he has studied the sacred books of his own religion. For doing so he makes references to personal reminiscences of his being attracted to Christ, Christianity and the Bible. The Christmas celebration in 1914 had great bearing on what Christ meant to him. He recalls it:

> On Christmas Eve we gathered before an altar on which a picture of the Madonna and Child had been placed ... While we were seated in silence, my master said: "Meditate on Christ within, and feel his living presence." An intense spiritual atmosphere pervaded the worship hall. Our minds were lifted up, and we felt ourselves transported into another consciousness. For the first time I realized that Christ was as much our own as Krishna ... Christ as a manifest expression of divinity I could never have considered foreign. But for a living and personal experience of him I needed the tangible heightening of consciousness resulting from the worship on that memorable Christmas Eve.[5]

Swami Prabhavananda regards this as his 'personal' experience of Christ. It was in the silent moment of meditation that he first encountered Christ. It filled his mind with the presence of Christ. This living presence later urged him to study Christ's teaching.

C. Swami Prabhavananda's interpretation of biblical texts

The evangelists Matthew and Luke place at the very start of Christ's public ministry a long discourse called the Sermon on the

York, 1972), p. xiii. To facilitate references within our text this work will be cited as Swami Prabhavananda, *Sermon on the Mount.*

[3] The story of Śrī Rāmakṛṣṇa's experience of Christ is told in: SHI, pp. 340-341.

[4] Cf. Swami Prabhavananda, *Sermon on the Mount,* p. xi.

[5] *Ibid.,* p. xii.

Mount. These two versions of the Sermon have many important similarities and dissimilarities. We do not see what has prompted Swami Prabhavananda to choose the version of Matthew for his study. Perhaps hȩ does not give any importance to the different traditions which reproduce the words of Christ; perhaps he finds an advantage of the numerous elements peculiar to Matthew's verson to explain the essence of Christian spirituality.

Swami Prabhavananda has attempted a spiritual interpretation of the Sermon on the Mount. For he finds its contents "uncompromisingly spiritual."[6] In it Christ taught the world the simple and profound truths of the "renunciation of worldliness, the contemplation of God, and the purification of the heart through the love of God."[7]

1. *Essentials of Christian Spirituality: Swami Prabhavananda's Interpretation of the Beatitudes*

Following Matthew word for word, Swami Prabhavananda introduces the discussion on the Beatitudes, from Mt 4:23 onwards, though they actually begin with Mt 5:3. Mt 5:3-11 enumerates nine beatitudes while its parallel text Lk 6:20-26 has four beatitudes and four maledictions. Swami Prabhavananda says that Christ did not want to give the Sermon on the Mount to the public; He gave it only to the chosen few. He did so because there is required in the spiritual aspirant a certain degree of spiritual fitness to receive the sublime truths of the Sermon. The first beatitude is a blessing to those who feel the spiritual need.

> "Blessed are the poor in spirit,
> for theirs is the kingdom of heaven" (Mt 5:3).

Matthew's expression "the poor in spirit"[8] Swami Prabhavananda interprets in the sense of the humble. He understands Christ's calling "the poor in spirit" blessed as one of the chief characteristics of Christian discipleship. In the interpretation of this beatitude we note that Swami Prabhavananda concentrates only on the general condition of Christ's discipleship, avoiding the polemics between material and spiritual poverty.

---

[6] *Ibid.,* p. xiv.
[7] *Ibid.*
[8] Luke simply puts it as "the poor" (Lk 6:20b).

"Blessed are those who mourn,
for they shall be comforted" (Mt 5:4).

Spiritual life begins with a desire to reach God. The first beatitude helps the disciple to make an assessment of the situation. As a result he understands that he has to make a long way before he can reach the goal. Then he is disposed to cry for the vision of God. This is a 'blessed' cry. Here what Swami Prabhavananda laments over is our "false sense of values." [9] That is to say, we are often satisfied with 'the surface life.' But this surface life will not give us peace and happiness which should be sought in God alone. He says: "When we begin to mourn as Christ wished us to mourn, when we shed even one tear for God, then we prepare the way for the comfort of that divine knowledge." [10]

"Blessed are the meek,
for they shall inherit the earth" (Mt 5:5).

The sense of ego stands behind many of the set-backs in spiritual life. Every time we try to assert our ego we go back from our goal of life, God-vision. Quite opposite is what Christ calls meekness. It is to live in self-surrender to God, free from the sense of 'me' and 'mine.' Christ calls them heirs of the earth who follow His teaching of meekness. As soon as we "give up our deluded individual claims, we find that in the truest sense everything belongs to us ..." [11] "By sincerely giving up the ego to God, by being meek, we will gain everything. We will inherit the earth." [12]

"Blessed are those who hunger and thirst for righteousness,
for they shall be satisfied" (Mt 5:6).

The fourth beatitude promises satisfaction to the hungry and the thirsty for righteousness. This hunger and thirst is evidently metaphorical; it expresses an ardent spiritual desire. Swami Prabhavananda says that in view of a number of passages in the Old Testament the righteousness for which Christ wants us to hunger and thirst is practically synonymous with salvation. He explains himself:

> This righteousness therefore is not what we ordinarily think of as moral virtues or good qualities, not relative good as opposed to evil,

[9] SWAMI PRABHAVANANDA, *Sermon on the Mount*, p. 20.
[10] *Ibid.*, p. 21.
[11] *Ibid.*, p. 22.
[12] *Ibid.*, p. 23.

or relative virtue as opposed to vice, but absolute righteousness, absolute goodness. The hunger and thirst after the righteousness of which Christ speaks is a hunger and thirst after God himself.[13]

He shows how we can intensify this hunger and thirst. In the beginning it may be a slight desire. Surely it can take us higher. We must start with prayer, worship and meditation. "As we practice these spiritual disciplines, our slight desire to realize him will become intensified until it is a raging hunger and a burning thirst." [14]

"Blessed are the merciful
for they shall obtain mercy" (Mt 5:7).

According to Swami Prabhavananda "to be merciful is one of the conditions necessary before we can receive the truth of God." [15] He explains this beatitude against the background of Yoga psychology, showing how its opposites — envy, jealousy and hatred — cause the spiritual edifice to collapse. Until these evil tendencies in our minds are wiped out we cannot even think of God. He concludes: "If we want to find God, we have to become God-like in mercy." [16]

"Blessed are the pure in heart,
for they shall see God" (Mt 5:8).

Swami Prabhavananda sets purity of heart, blessed by Christ in this beatitude, in the general context of the great world religions. According to him all the religions have two basic principles: the ideal to be realized and the method of its realization. He says that in the Sermon on the Mount the ideal is to be perfect as the Father in heaven; and the method is the purification of the heart.

According to him Christ's call to be pure in heart is not merely to be pure in an ethical sense. Ethical life is a preparation for spiritual life; yet it does not bring God-vision. "It is like the foundation of a house; it is not the superstructure." [17]

---

[13] *Ibid.*, pp. 23-24.

[14] *Ibid.*, p. 24. In this connection Swami Prabhavananda quotes Śrī Rāmakṛṣṇa who described the way to find God as follows: "Longing is like the rosy dawn. After the dawn, out comes the sun. Longing is followed by the vision of God ... The point is, to love God even as a mother loves her child, the chaste wife her husband, and the worldly man his wealth. Add together these three forces of love, these three powers of attraction, and give it all to God. Then you will certainly see Him." *Gospel*, p. 7.

[15] SWAMI PRABHAVANANDA, *Sermon on the Mount*, p. 25.

[16] *Ibid.*

[17] *Ibid.*, p. 26.

He then speaks of the test of purity. If we try to meditate on God and if it moves uninterruptedly, it means that we are already pure in heart; if we think about everything except God, it means that the mind is still impure.

There are many ways to purify the heart. Christ teaches them throughout the Sermon. Most important of all is devotion to God. "The more we think of the Lord and take refuge in him, the more we shall love him — and the purer our hearts will become." [18]

> "Blessed are the peacemakers,
> for they shall be called sons of God" (Mt 5:9).

Swami Prabhavananda interprets this beatitude in the light of transcendental consciousness. In that state we are conscious of our status as the children of God and peacemakers. "We cannot bring peace until we have realized our oneness with God and with all beings." [19] But even in the ordinary consciousness the disciple has to be a peacemaker. When a man has a real spiritual orientation God becomes manifest in his heart. In seeing him other people feel a spiritual joy. Therefore, Christ's saying that the peacemakers are blessed is verifiable even in this life.

The last two beatitudes, namely blessings to the persecuted for justice and for Christ, Swami Prabhavananda sees as one whole and interprets as such.

> "Blessed are those who are persecuted for righteousness' sake, for theirs is the kingdom of heaven.
> "Blessed are you when men revile you and persecute you and utter all kinds of evil against you falsely on my account" (Mt 5:10-11).

Persecution is the inevitable lot of Christ's disciples. For worldly people do not understand the value of spiritual life. When they see that the spiritual man does not conform to their ideals they insult him and do him harm. Nevertheless he does not react. For his mind is fixed on God.

No really spiritual man will do anything in order to please others. Rather he prefers to please God even if the whole world is against him. Persecution comes in this way.

Swami Prabhavananda now describes the attitude of a spiritual man in front of his persecutors. Feelings of resentment and retaliation

---

[18] *Ibid.*, p. 28.
[19] *Ibid.*, p. 29.

harm not only the adversaries but also oneself. In giving in to these feelings the spiritual man makes himself unfit for meditation on God. Christ who prayed on the cross for His adversaries is the ideal.

The reward in heaven waits for the persecuted. Since for Swami Prabhavananda heaven is within, the reward is immediate. Thus the illumined soul, always absorbed in God, feels the presence of God within, even in this life. He transcends physical consciousness even while living on earth.

What we have seen in the preceding pages is Swami Prabhavananda's interpretation of the Beatitudes. While it may be lacking in the scholarship of a Bible commentator, nevertheless, it gives evidence of the profound vision of a spiritual master.

2. *Symbols of the Christian Spiritual Man: Salt of the Earth and Light of the World*

Immediately after the Beatitudes Christ has spoken four verses (Mt 5:13-16) which serve as a transition between the Beatitudes and their development in the rest of the Sermon on the Mount. These four verses constitute a single unit introduced by two parallel declarations: "You are the salt of the earth ... You are the light of the world ..." Swami Prabhavananda separately discusses these two statements of Christ.

The illustration of the salt, like that of the light, in our view, could mean that Christ's disciples are to undertake a benevolent role in the world, which they have to fulfil chiefly through their character and example. The accent seems to be on what they have to be for others.

Swami Prabhavananda does not stress this aspect of Christ's illustration. Instead he speaks of it from another perspective. For him Christ is an ideal spiritual master who attentively studies the personality of His disciples and helps them to develop it in the right direction. Declaring them to be the salt of the earth, He instils in them a firm faith in themselves and a feeling that weakness, cowardice and failure have no part in their true nature. The perfect spiritual master, Christ, can see into the heart of His disciples. He does not condemn them for their faults and weaknesses; He knows human nature; He knows that the disciples cannot grow spiritually if they lack self-confidence.

Swami Prabhavananda observes that this self-confidence and the beatitude promised to the meek are not in contradiction. Rather they harmonize in a spiritual man. For according to him, calling His disciples 'the salt of the earth,' Christ was referring not to their lower self but was trying to instil in them a faith in the higher Self, God within.[20]

The second illustration, that of the light, shows that it is not enough to evoke self-confidence in the disciples; the teacher must be able to transmit spirituality. A truly spiritual man, having obtained illumination through union with God, illumines the hearts of his disciples. Thus, for Swami Prabhavananda this spiritual power is a sign of divine commission. "Religion degenerates when taught by unillumined men." [21] The principle behind this is: "In order to transform people's lives, one must first light one's own candle." [22]

Having explained the role of Jesus as master, Swami Prabhavananda tries to explain that the disciples themselves have to be light of the world. The very presence of a spiritual man is a blessing to society. People who approach him are "susceptible to a spiritual atmosphere" and "cannot help thinking of God and loving him." [23] From his own experience he says that in the presence of Śrī Rāmakṛṣṇa's disciples there was an intense feeling that God-realization was easy. Because in their presence people felt the presence of God Himself.

3. *Conditions of Christian Existence*

To become Christ's disciple a total transformation of a person is necessary. Christ calls every man to become perfect like the Father. According to Swami Prabhavananda this perfection is the last of a series of three steps leading progressively to God-realization. We shall see each of them briefly.

a) Spiritual Rebirth (Jn 3:3-6)

One of the Biblical texts to which Swami Prabhavananda attaches profound significance from a theological and spiritual viewpoint is the following:

> Jesus answered him [Nicode'mus], "Truly, truly, I say to you, unless one is born anew, he cannot see the kingdom of God." Nicode'mus

---

20 Cf. *ibid.*, p. 37.
21 *Ibid.*, p. 38.
22 *Ibid.*, p. 39.
23 *Ibid.*, p. 40.

said to him, "How can a man be born when he is old? Can he enter a second time into his mother's womb and be born?" Jesus answered, "Truly, truly, I say to you, unless one is born of water and the Spirit, he cannot enter the kingdom of God. That which is born of the flesh is flesh, and that which is born of the Spirit is spirit" (Jn 3:3-6).

In many places he quotes this text, sometimes fully and at other times partially, or makes references to it, to the effect that in his understanding of Christian spirituality it is a cardinal point. For 'the possibility of achieving spiritual rebirth is central in the Gospel of Christ.' [24]

But except in two places where he quotes the text in full,[25] he speaks only of rebirth in the spirit, whereas Christ says: "unless one is born of *water and the Spirit ...*" This text is pointed out by theologians as one of the most important texts in the New Testament on Baptism. We cannot affirm that by the omission of 'birth of water' he purposefully avoids any reference to Christ's teaching on Baptism. Even though he speaks of a birth in the spirit, the spirit he speaks of is not the Holy Spirit of the Trinity. In fact he does not speak of the spirit as a particular person in the mysterious life of God. In his writings birth in the spirit can be understood as a spiritual awakening, a superconscious experience or a renewal of the mind.

Swami Prabhavananda emphasizes the connection between the new birth and the vision of the kingdom of God.[26] He presents the new birth as being absolutely indispensable for seeing the kingdom of God and attaining life eternal. Evidently by seeing he means realization. And this is possible in this very life. According to him when Christ said "unless a man is born anew, he cannot see the kingdom of God," He was not denying every value in the present life. This life is necessary in order that we may transcend it. The new birth does not take place at death. "We must struggle to be born in spirit, to attain superconscious knowledge in this very life." [27]

In one place Swami Prabhavananda reflects on this 'birth in spirit' from the viewpoint of evolution.[28] In the mineral kingdom there is life and consciousness although they are covered by matter.

---

[24] Cf. Swami Prabhavananda, SHI, p. 184.
[25] Cf. *ibid.* Cf. also Swami Prabhavananda, RP, p. 196.
[26] Cf. *ibid.,* p. 34.
[27] *Ibid.*
[28] Cf. *ibid.,* pp. 60-61.

In the vegetable kingdom matter predominates, but there is a certain degree of expression of life and consciousness. In man there is an unfolding of the two, but man too is not free from matter. It is only in Christ and other illumined souls there is an infinite expression of the infinite consciousness. They transcend the sense of ego which limits the infinite consciousness in man. He says: "To transcend this ego and unfold the infinite consciousness is what Christ would call the birth in spirit." [29]

Swami Prabhavananda understands Christ's saying "and you will know the truth, and the truth will make you free" (Jn 8:32) as an invitation to everyone to realize God as Christ Himself did. The experience of this truth is made possible through spiritual rebirth. He identifies this new birth with what the Upaniṣads call the 'Fourth.' [30] "Christians call it the mystical union," says he.[31] He asks: "What does it mean to have Christ born in our hearts? It is to come face to face with God and thereby to attain perfection. That is the one purpose of religion." [32]

We Christians believe that this birth in spirit is a genuine becoming. The very use of the verb "to be born" suggests a radical conversion. It is an entirely new life. "To be born of the Spirit" is to be born to a new life, a new way of being and acting. St. Paul taught that the principle of this regeneration is the Spirit (Rm 8: 16-17). In the Spirit the believer undergoes a great transformation — from a carnal man to a spiritual man. Entirely docile to the movements of the Spirit, he is "born of the Spirit." This rebirth, Swami Prabhavananda notices, is the death of the ego. For he asks to "die the death of the ego and be reborn spiritually, even in this life." [33]

---

[29] *Ibid.*, p. 61. Here Swami Prabhavananda equates the infinite consciousness with God.

[30] Cf. BU 5.14.1-3; Mā U 7; Maitrī U 6.19; 7.11. Although the Sanskrit word *turīya* literally means the 'Fourth,' yet it has no numerical significance. Swami Prabhavananda identifies the 'Fourth' with transcendental consciousness and regards it as the supreme mystical experience. He says that it is realized when in meditation the ego is left behind and there is a full manifestation of the true Self. Cf. SWAMI PRABHAVANANDA, SHI, p. 54.

[31] ID., *Sermon on the Mount,* p. 73.

[32] ID., RP, p. 89.

[33] *Ibid.*, p. 172.

b) "Follow me" (Lk 18:22)

"Follow me," says Christ to His disciples; and His call, full of authority, makes them the messengers of His Word (Mk 1:17-20; 2:14). Once they begin to follow Him, they are going to be initiated into the mystery of His divine life. To follow Christ is not only to follow His teaching, but to share His life as well. His life was not only an event of glory, but also of passion and cross. Christ demands abnegation, total detachment from riches, departure from relatives (Mt 8:20-22; 10:37) without looking back (Lk 9:62). This is Christ's call; but not all respond to it (Lk 18:23).

Swami Prabhavananda, however, tries to explain the meaning of Christ's call to follow Him differently. He analyses Lk 18:18-22 and then asks: "What did Christ mean when he said, 'Follow me?' He meant renunciation of all attachments and devotion to God alone." [34]

The renunciation which, according to Swami Prabhavananda, is the meaning of Christ's "follow me" is indeed "the beginning, the middle, and the end of spiritual life." [35] Christ is one of its greatest exponents.[36] For He taught: "He who loves his life loses it, and he who hates his life in this world will keep it for eternal life" (Jn 12:25). Swami Prabhavananda says that the Christians who misunderstand Hinduism for its ideal of renunciation as 'life-negating,' forget the teaching of their own master.[37]

According to Swami Prabhavananda Christ's "follow me" is echoed in the Sermon on the Mount too. For did not Christ ask His followers to enter by the narrow gate? (Mt 7:13-14). Explaining the meaning of the "narrow gate," he asks for great struggle to follow Christ. Christ warns to check the natural human tendency to rush out through the wide gates of the senses. At the same time people who hesitate to enter by the "narrow gate" miss a lot of life's bliss. "They do not realize that what a joy and freedom there is in spiritual life." [38] In another place commenting on Christ's saying: "For my yoke is easy, and my burden is light" (Mt 11:30), he says: "the ordinary undiscriminating life of sense-attachment is really much

---

[34] *Ibid.*, p. 65.

[35] SWAMI PRABHAVANANDA, SHI, p. 100.

[36] Cf. ID., "The Ideal of Renunciation," in: *Vedanta for the Western World*, p. 269.

[37] Cf. ID., RP, p. 153.

[38] *Ibid.*, p. 138.

more painful, much harder to bear, than the disciplines which will set us free." [39] For from His disciples who are to spread His teaching Christ does not ask to give up anything but selfishness, the denial of 'me' and 'mine' and the conversion of the lust of the flesh into love of God.

We agree that the ideal of renunciation is essential to Christ's "follow me." Indeed He made it very clear, saying: "If any man would come after me, let him deny himself and take up his cross and follow me" (Mt 16:24). But renunciation does not exhaust all the aspects of Christ's call to discipleship. To follow Christ necessitates a total attachment and an absolute submission to Him, that is to say, faith and obedience. It is to have faith in Him, a faith which relies on His Word alone. But Swami Prabhavananda does not make any explicit reference to this aspect of "follow me." It is, in fact, faith that overcomes the hesitations during one's following Christ.

The following of Christ radically changes the disciple. He thinks and acts differently and is spontaneously led to fulfil Christ's demand to become perfect like the Father.

c) 'Be perfect' (Mt 5:48)

A phrase of the Gospel gives as the model of perfection; the very perfection of the heavenly Father: "You, therefore, must be perfect, as your heavenly Father is perfect" (Mt 5:48). In this sentence Swami Prabhavananda sees "the central theme of the Sermon on the Mount" [40] and "the whole purpose of man's life." [41]

But what is meant by perfection? He believes that as long as we are in the world of relativity we cannot have an adequate idea of perfection. For perfection is absolute. He criticizes theologians who interpret the perfection which Christ taught as a relative perfection, toward which we always grow but never fully achieve. He believes that Christ did not mean that. Christ said definitely, 'be perfect.' "Perfection," he says, "to be perfection, must be an absolute perfection, nothing less." [42] But we have to note here that his idea of perfection is hardly tenable except in the Advaitic perspective.

He teaches that this perfection is the divine heritage of man.

---

[39] Swami Prabhavananda on *Yoga-sūtra* I.12-15.
[40] Id., *Sermon on the Mount,* p. 69.
[41] Id., RP, p. 87.
[42] *Ibid.,* p. 144.

Commenting upon St. Paul's teaching that we are privileged to call God "Abba! Father!" and that this raises us to the status of children and heirs (Rm 8:16-17), he says: "We have the right to aspire to that perfection ..." [43]

This perfection is to be attained here and now. He holds that Christ's call to perfection and the Upaniṣadic teaching that one has to know the Reality here converge on one point: "What we have to earn we must earn here on earth. We must reach the unitive knowledge of Godhead and enjoy the bliss of heaven even in this life." [44] He affirms that in asking His disciples to become perfect, Christ did not mean that only after having died a physical death could they attain that perfection.

Where is this perfection to be sought? He says that Christ refers to a transcendental wisdom, which is the unitive knowledge of man's true being as one with God. "To uncover this true being, or divinity, which lies hidden within oneself, is to become perfect." [45] Here it would have been desirable if he associated perfection with love (*agapê*) existing in God and the believer. The love operative in man is a participation in God's love; it is even that love given to him. So profound is his union with God that he can now say with St. Paul "... it is no longer I who live, but Christ who lives in me ..." (Gal 2:20). But since Swami Prabhavananda is an Advaitin who prefers 'union in knowledge' to 'union in love,' he finds the ideal of perfection in the direct and immediate knowledge of the Absolute.[46]

And finally, Swami Prabhavananda asks why only a few individuals reach perfection. Because few care to seek for it. Most people remain content with living a more or less ethical life. But Christ's 'be ye perfect' makes no exception. He regrets: "Christ's ideal of perfection is generally either forgotten or misunderstood. True, many people read the Sermon on the Mount, but few try to live its teachings." [47] They may be intellectually convinced of becoming perfect as the Father; but their hearts do not respond. He affirms that, whatever the theologians may say to the contrary, Christ taught that man can and should be as perfect as God Himself. He expresses this by saying:

---

[43] SWAMI PRABHAVANANDA, *Sermon on the Mount,* p. 70.
[44] ID., RP, p. 60. The reference is to Kena U 13(5).
[45] ID., *Sermon on the Mount,* p. 71.
[46] Cf. ID., RP, p. 198.
[47] ID., *Sermon on the Mount,* p. 73.

> But this much I can say — that when Christ spoke to his disciples he meant literally that God could be seen in their present lives. And the disciples were hungering just for that truth, to know God, to be perfect even as the Father is perfect.[48]

His criticism is directed against theologians who hope to satisfy the neophytes who hunger and thirst after God-vision, with theology, philosophy and doctrines. This statement, although exaggerated, has some truth in it. For there is a temptation to believe that it is possible to encompass God in a system of theology. The great saints and the genuine believers did not fall into it; quite the contrary. But this tendency has seriously diminished the meditative experience in Christianity.

In the above pages we have selected those passages in the Gospels which Swami Prabhavananda interprets as containing the essential aspects of Christian spirituality. A selection became necessary since they were not directly concerned with meditation, the subject of our study. In the following, and also the last, part of this chapter we shall try to expose his interpretation of Christian meditation.

D. Christian meditation

In Swami Prabhavananda's idea of religion the inner core of every religion consists in the personal experience of the truth of God. Therefore man's greatest preoccupation should be to experience God for himself. And what is the means thereof? The impact of meditation on spiritual experiences is undeniable. No religion can do without the practice of meditation. The fact that Hinduism puts emphasis on meditation does not mean that it is foreign to other religions. Quoting St. Paul who taught the Christians to "pray constantly," [49] Swami Prabhavananda says that meditation is fundamental in Christianity as well.

We now propose to reproduce two meditations, one on Christ and the other on the Our Father, which according to Swami Prabhavananda exhibit the chief elements of Christian meditation.

---

[48] *Ibid.*

[49] I Thes 5:17. "Pray at all times in the Spirit, with all prayer and supplication ..." (Eph 6:18); "... be constant in prayer" (Rm 12:12).

1. *Meditation on Christ*

In our view, the mysteries of Christ offer the Christian infinite possibilities for meditation. Faith guarantees him that he can reach God in Christ. For Christ says that he who sees Him, sees the Father (Jn 14:9) and that He and the Father are one (Jn 10:30). Therefore faith is all-important. The Christ of Christian faith is very different from what He means to Swami Prabhavananda.[50] Hence the contents and ways of meditation of a Christian are also different from what he proposes. However he attaches great importance to meditation on Christ.

In the beginning of this chapter we saw how Swami Prabhavananda meditated on Christ and had the experience of His living presence, which he later confessed to be his first personal encounter with Christ. In his commentary on the *Yoga-sūtras* he proposes a similar meditation on Christ. Patañjali said that concentration may be attained "by meditating on the heart of an illumined soul, that is free from passion" (YS I.37). Here Swami Prabhavananda specifies the role of meditation on the heart of Christ. He recommends trying to "imagine how it must *feel* to be a great saint."[51] This practice develops the emotive life of the meditant. He feels a kind of union with Christ. He begins to think, feel and love as Christ Himself would have thought, felt and loved. He now feels to be transformed into the person of Christ and that Christ's heart has become his. That it is not true and proper meditation we admit. But according to Swami Prabhavananda this localization of the image is very

---

[50] Swami Prabhavananda respects Christ and esteems His teaching. Next to the great teachers of his own religion it is Christ who has influenced him most. To him Christ is a spiritual teacher, one of the great prophets of the world, an associate of God (*Īśvarakoti*), but above all an *avatār*. This is perhaps the greatest tribute which as a Hindu he can ever pay to Christ. An *avatār* in Hinduism means a descent of God. One may find similarities as well as differences between the Hindu doctrine of *avatāra* and the mystery of Christ's incarnation. An important difference between the two doctrines is to be found in BG 4.6-8, where Kṛṣṇa says that he consorts with Nature which is his, and comes into being in this age and in that. That is to say, Hinduism admits plurality of God's descent. Swami Prabhavananda justifies this Hindu view and holds that the same God who came as Kṛṣṇa and Buddha came again as Christ. Although he shows willingness to accept Christ as an *avatār,* the Christian teaching that Christ is the only Son of God, the only incarnate God, is not acceptable to him. He expresses his attitude to Christ as follows: "Now as a Hindu, and especially as a follower of Ramakrishna, I can say that I accept Jesus Christ wholeheartedly, but I do not accept Him as the *only* incarnation of God." SWAMI PRABHAVANANDA, RP, p. 51.

[51] SWAMI PRABHAVANANDA on *Yoga-sūtra* I.37.

helpful to beginners in meditation. Those who find it difficult to concentrate may profit from this kind of localization.

Meditation on Christ according to Swami Prabhavananda is the effort to live our life in Christ.[52] In order to meditate on Christ the spiritual seeker should gradually try to centre his whole life on Christ. This is a new form of life. Christ becomes the centre of his life. Although Swami Prabhavananda's use of faith in Christ is not in the Christian sense there is a constant call to feel His presence. "Christ is your own *Atman,* the Self within." [53] When the believer has begun to let his consciousness flow into the life and teaching of Christ he will feel a tangible presence of Christ and will realize that he thinks and acts and breathes because of that presence within him and everywhere.[54]

Within this perspective he gives another meditation on Christ. It appears in his commentary on Patañjali: "In that samādhi [nirvicāra samādhi], knowledge is said to be 'filled with truth' " (YS I.48). He explains how in *nirvicāra samādhi* the mind is said to become "pure" and "filled with truth." The mind is said to become pure, because what makes it impure, the various thought-waves, are swallowed by one great wave of concentration on a single object. Christ is here regarded as a chosen ideal, the single object of concentration. When all the thought-waves of the mind are made to give way to a great thought-wave of concentration on Christ, the meditant will experience direct contact with Him. This contact between Christ and the meditant is no longer "something subjectively imagined, but as something objectively known." [55] It happens in the following way: if the spiritual aspirant has been meditating on Christ, and trying to picture Him to himself in his imagination, he finds that his picture dissolves into the reality of a living presence. In the experience of that presence he realizes that his imagination of Christ was imperfect. Swami Prabhavananda likens this experience of divine grace to the action of a magnet. The beginner in meditation may have to struggle hard to keep the mind on Christ from its wandering thoughts. But if he perseveres in his attempt to fix it on the person of Christ he will soon feel a help from above. Like

---

52 Cf. Id., RP, p. 215.
53 *Ibid.,* p. 166.
54 Cf. *ibid.,* pp. 135-136.
55 Swami Prabhavananda on *Yoga-sūtra* I.48.

a magnet his object of concentration, in this case Christ, will attract him and lead him in the desired direction.

According to Swami Prabhavananda meditation is a wrestling with the spirit.[56] Lazy people cannot meditate. For meditation requires ardent desire to reach God and strenuous effort to concentrate the mind. It is in this sense that he says meditation is an unbroken flow of thought toward God. In other words, the meditant should feel to be enveloped by the constant presence of God. When the mind is established in the constant union with God, the stage of meditation is described as constant recollectedness.[57] To reach this state the meditator must acquire a certain degree of purity of mind and detachment from sense-objects. For this purpose he suggests a meditation on Christ. The present meditation comes in his commentary on the *Yoga-sūtras* I.51.

This meditation on Christ has three successive stages. The first stage begins with the gross phenomena. Here the meditant approaches Christ as a human being. He tries to know about His life as much as he can do. As a result he begins to love Christ; love, when intensified, becomes an urge to be like Christ; he seeks to serve Christ and resolves to spread His message and models his life upon Him. "Through this service and this love non-attachment to other, lesser loves and objects comes naturally." [58]

In the second stage Christ is not meditated upon as a human being; He is an *avatār*. It is a passage from the gross phenomena to the spiritual one. This passage is made possible through devotion to Christ and meditation upon Him. The divine aspect becomes prominent in this stage.

Higher indeed is the third stage, the stage of consciousness. Here Christ transcends even the state of *avatār*. For behind Him is the Supreme God, the ultimate Reality of which He is but a partial, individual representation. When meditation on Christ deepens, then in the stage of consciousness the meditant is:

> united with That which was manifested in Christ and hidden within our unregenerate selves, but which is eternally present in all of us. And this union is the state of nirvikalpa samadhi.[59]

---

[56] Cf. Id., RP, p. 190.
[57] Cf. *ibid.,* p. 146.
[58] Swami Prabhavananda on *Yoga-sūtra* I.51.
[59] *Ibid.*

From what we have so far seen it is clear that for Swami Prabhavananda meditation on Christ is not as high and sublime as the Advaitic meditation on the formless Absolute. All the same beginners in the spiritual life derive much benefit from it. The emphasis falls on the aspect of personal encounter with Christ through meditation. His advice is to 'find Christ within your own heart.' The way to this discovery is meditation on Christ.

2. *Meditation on the Lord's Prayer*

From the two traditions on the teaching of the 'Our Father,'[60] Swami Prabhavananda has chosen the Matthean tradition for his meditation, beacuse in Matthew the Our Father is integrated into the Sermon on the Mount. He prefers to call it "The Lord's Prayer" and thinks it is "the best known prayer in the world." [61] For in it "Jesus teaches us how to become absorbed in the consciousness of God." [62] Hence he grants it the value of a meditative prayer.

The prayer begins

"Our Father"

Genuine prayer establishes a certain type of relationship with God. According to Swami Prabhavananda, in calling God our Father "Christ is teaching us how to think of God when we pray to him." [63] God is the object of meditation. But "God as an impersonal being is too abstract to meditate upon." [64] Referring to Christ's teaching "You shall love the Lord your God with all your heart, and with all your soul, and with all your strength, and with all your mind" (Lk 10:27), he says that to fulfil this commandment we have to enter into a definite relationship with God.[65] Everyone knows the love of a father, or a mother, or a friend or a beloved. These expressions of relationship, existing on the human plane, may also be established with God.

Swami Prabhavananda holds that these relationships with God, characteristic of the *bhakti* sects in Hindu religion, are not its sole

---

[60] Mt 6:9-13 = Lk 11:2-4.
[61] SWAMI PRABHAVANANDA, *Sermon on the Mount,* p. 84.
[62] *Ibid.*, p. 85.
[63] *Ibid.*
[64] *Ibid.*
[65] Cf. *ibid.*

patrimony; Christians also are familiar with them.[66] To Jesus God was a Father. The Wise men of the East adored God as the child Jesus. Christ addressed His disciples as friends. Some of the great Christian mystics looked on themselves as God's servants. He concludes:

> In the Lord's Prayer, however, and in many other of Christ's teachings, we are told to think of God as our Father, whom we many regard partly with reverence, but chiefly with trust, absolute confidence, and love.[67]

God who is addressed as our Father is

"in heaven"

In Christ's instruction on prayer there is a comparison between the earthly father and the heavenly Father (Mt 7:9-11). Christ said to " call no man your father on earth, for you have one Father, who is in heaven" (Mt 23:9). While Luke uses the expression "the heavenly Father" (Lk 11:13), Matthew speaks of the "Father who art in heaven" (Mt 6:9), and "your Father who is in heaven" (Mt 7:11). But Swami Prabhavananda understands this expression as the human mind's search to find proofs of God's existence.[68] He agrees that the arguments of philosophers and theologians, demonstrating the existence of God, may be logically valid. But the argument from the design as found in the teleological side of Christian theology is "neither very convincing nor very important." [69] For the opponents' arguments are not logically invalid. Therefore according to him:

> ... there is only one way to verify the actuality of God, and that is to see him for oneself. All attempts to arrive at a proof by means of reasoning are futile, because what we are trying to establish is only the existence of our *idea* of God. Hence, even if we could possibly make such a proof, how could we guarantee that our idea and the reality of God would correspond? [70]

No amount of proof for the existence of God will carry conviction that God is. The real proof is to experience Him. Until

---

[66] Cf. *ibid.*, p. 86; SWAMI PRABHAVANANDA on *Yoga-sūtra* II.45; ID., SHI, p. 330n.

[67] SWAMI PRABHAVANANDA, *Sermon on the Mount*, p. 86.

[68] Cf. *ibid.*

[69] SWAMI PRABHAVANANDA, SHI, p. 205.

[70] ID., *Sermon on the Mount*, p. 87.

one can say 'God exists; I know, because I have seen Him,' God does not exist for him. Hence to say that God is in heaven is to realize Him in one's own consciousness. Many do not see heaven in their own consciousness because they are filled with earth-consciousness. Meditation on the "Father who is in heaven" should purify the mind, free it from the attachment of the world and open the eye of the Spirit.

"Hallowed be thy name"

In asking us to pray for the glory of God's name Christ, according to Swami Prabhavananda, puts emphasis upon the name of God. The name of God in itself is of the greatest religious significance. In order to establish that the name of God is hallowed not only in Hinduism but also in Christianity, he cites the following Biblical texts:

Ps 103:1	Bless the LORD, O my soul; and all that is within me, bless his holy name!
Jn 16:23-24	... Truly, truly, I say to you, if you ask anything of the Father, he will give it to you in my name. Hitherto you have asked nothing in my name; ask, and you will receive, that your joy may be full.
Rm 10:13	For every one who calls upon the name of the Lord will be saved.
Hb 13:15	Through him then let us continually offer up a sacrifice of praise to God, that is, the fruit of lips that acknowledge his name.

He associates the Hindu concept of *mantra* with 'Word was God' of Jn 1:1.[71] *Mantra* is God's name. He takes 'Hail Mary' as a *mantra*.[72] Although 'Hail Mary' is not God's name it is someway related to it and can be used for prayer and meditation. Another Christian *mantra* is 'Lord Jesus Christ, have mercy on us' practised in the Eastern Orthodox Church.

Constant repetition of God's name together with meditation on the same empties the mind of all its worldly cravings and attachments. At a certain stage the devotee may experience God's name as living and conscious, illuminating his consciousness. How this comes about Swami Prabhavananda explains as follows:

---

71 Cf. *ibid.*, p. 89.
72 Cf. *ibid.*, p. 90.

> As the name of God is repeated, the spiritual power with which it is charged becomes evident. By hallowing the Name over and over again, we let God take possession of our conscious minds so that finally, no matter what we are doing or saying or thinking, some part of our minds will be praising him.[73]

Again, the Lord's Prayer is God-centred. For the devotee prays

"Thy kingdom come"

According to Swami Prabhavananda this is not a hope for the future. For the kingdom of God has already come. Referring to Christ's saying "the kingdom of heaven is at hand" (Mt 3:2), he accuses lazy Christians of desiring to postpone its advent. Why we do not see it existent here is that our divine sight has been lost in worldly concern. He says:

> ... Christ tells us that God's kingdom has come already; it has always been with us and we must realize this. At least when we pray and meditate we should forget this universe, forget ourselves, and feel that God alone exists. Through such practice ... we will actually see his kingdom in our hearts and all around us.[74]

"Thy will be done,
On earth as it is in heaven"

Swami Prabhavananda knows the importance of doing the will of God. A genuine devotee of God, having surrendered his ego to God, finds it easy to know God's will and implement it. But how can one discern God's will in a given situation? There are people who do exactly what they want to do, claiming that it is God's will. Until one is spiritually illumined, one cannot know for certain what God wants of him. But there is a way to distinguish between what is God's will and what is our will. Swami Prabhavananda asks: "Do you feel the presence of God and remember him? If you do something and consider it God's will and have forgotten God, then you may be sure it is your own will." [75] The only criterion, therefore, is to do what leads us to God. What leads us away from Him is certainly not His will.

"Give us this day our daily bread"

---

[73] *Ibid.,* p. 89.
[74] *Ibid.,* p. 92.
[75] SWAMI PRABHAVANANDA, RP, p. 246.

Prayer for "our daily bread" according to Swami Prabhavananda means prayer for the bread of divine grace.[76] In the Lord's Prayer the devotee prays that God's grace may be revealed to him now, this day, and for ever. This revelation may come at any time. We must patiently wait for it.

Swami Prabhavananda connects the mystery of salvation with the mystery of divine grace. People may practise asceticism with the hope of attaining God. This is pure vanity. For "Our own struggles will never make us pure or bring us the sight of God. No one can buy God with spiritual practices." [77] It is not right to believe that mystical states could be produced at will, provided one used the appropriate means. Human efforts can bring about certain states, but these states cannot be said to give God-vision. The spiritual aspirant is not left to his own capabilities. It is God who gives him the strength to search for Him. And anyone who tries to lift himself up to God is deceiving himself. Swami Prabhavananda examines Christ's words to His disciples: "You did not choose me, but I chose you ..." (Jn 15:16). From this saying of Jesus he arrives at the necessity of divine grace.

If God's grace is necessary for salvation, why do not all receive it? Is God partial in giving His grace? Swami Prabhavananda answers: "God's grace is always upon us; but self-effort and spiritual disciplines are necessary in order that we may become receptive to it." [78] Christ said:

> Watch therefore — for you do not know when the master of the house will come, in the evening, or at midnight, or at cockcrow, or in the morning — lest he come suddenly and find you asleep. And what I say to you I say to all: Watch (Mk 13:35-37).

Here Christ is demanding constant vigilance on the part of His disciples. This constant vigilance is nothing but meditation. For Swami Prabhavananda says: "We must be watchful; we must struggle to fix the mind on God in prayer and meditation." [79] But even when we persist in our efforts, we must not forget that they have value only through God's grace which animates and guides them. All our strength is in the strength of God.

---

[76] Cf. Id., *Sermon on the Mount,* p. 93.
[77] *Ibid.,* p. 94.
[78] *Ibid.*
[79] *Ibid.*

"And forgive us our debts,
As we have forgiven our debtors"

Swami Prabhavananda reads the "debts" in this prayer as the debts of *karma.* This doctrine means that every thought or action has its inevitable consequences. The doer alone is responsible for the consequences of his actions. He says that we must recognize our debts, that what we undergo at present has been earned by ourselves, that we should not hold any one else responsible for what we may suffer.[80] Only then can we hope that God will forgive us our debts.

The prayer ends with the plea

"And lead us not into temptation,
But deliver us from evil"

Swami Prabhavananda says that many people may find it difficult to understand this part of the Lord's Prayer. For how can God be said to lead us into temptation? But for him, it is easier to understand this petition as it is presented. He sees the whole world as a gigantic temptation to forget God. Led by the cravings of the ego, a man may try to remain content with something in the place of God.

In this connection Swami Prabhavananda sees an allegory of the temptation of *māyā* in the story of the Garden of Eden.[81] Adam is the symbol of Ātman, Eve the intellect of Adam and the serpent *māyā.* As Eve yields to temptation Adam also falls. He forgets his divine nature and experiences the vicissitudes of life.

"Deliver us from evil" means to be freed from the snares of the ego-feeling. Swami Prabhavananda says: "we must restrain the outgoing senses and turn within, where God dwells; we must take refuge in God and pray for divine grace." [82]

3. *Conclusion*

We shall conclude this chapter with the following observations:

1. Christ ends His Sermon on the Mount with the appeal to build the house upon a rock (Mt 7:24-25). Christ, according to Swami Prabhavananda, is here saying that one must lay the foundation

[80] Cf. *ibid.,* p. 95.
[81] Cf. *ibid.,* p. 97.
[82] *Ibid.*

of the spiritual edifice on the rock of spiritual experience. This is the experience of God received in meditation.

2. With regard to the meditation on Christ there is a very clear indication that Swami Prabhavananda develops it in the form of the loving meditation. Elsewhere he admits the various forms of divine love, taught by the *bhakti* schools of Hinduism, also in Christianity. Therefore we could naturally expect him to use these different types of love in the meditation on Christ. But this is absent here and we are left without any explanation.

3. We see also a difference between Christian meditation in Swami Prabhavananda and the meditation of Patañjali. Patañjali's technique of meditation consists in concentrating on a single thought. But in the meditation on the 'Our Father', for example, we have dwelt on many aspects of Christ's teachings. And it is truly meditation in so far as we have not moved from the central point.

4. Swami Prabhavananda is critical with regard to the Christian practice of meditation. The Western mind has no justification in saying that it cannot meditate. All its progress in the field of experimental sciences proves to the contrary. The fact is that it has concentrated on material progress, disregarding the hunger for spiritual life. Therefore, he says that contemporary Christians have forgotten the original teaching of Christ. For them the idea of contemplation has lost its significance and consequently the religion taught by Christ is nearly forgotten.[83]

[83] Cf. Swami Prabhavananda, RP, pp. 223-224.

Chapter VI

EVALUATION AND CONCLUSION

At the conclusion of chapter five, we noted the direction to be taken in understanding Christian meditation by way of comparing it to Hindu practice. According to Swami Prabhavananda's interpretation of Biblical texts, it is the over-application of reason in spirituality that has impoverished Christian meditation. The present chapter develops a synthesis of Hindu-Christian meditation in four phases: (1) Swami Prabhavananda's understanding of Hindu meditation, (2) Swami Prabhavananda's understanding of Christian meditation, (3) What is Christian meditation? (4) A Christian way of Hindu meditation.

A. Swami Prabhavananda on Hindu meditation

1. *Meditation as the Way to the Experience of God*

The ultimate truth with regard to man and his true nature has been declared by the seers of the Upaniṣads in such statements as "That thou art" and "I am Brahman." These are known as 'great utterances.' Swami Prabhavananda regards them as revealed truths.[1] The great sages, in a state of illumination, were blessed with a direct experience of these truths. But it would be wrong on our part if we did not follow the methods shown by them, and tried to understand them by the aid of human intellect alone, instead of realizing the truth for ourselves. In other words, the ultimate criterion of the truth of the great sayings is personal experiment and experience of their contents.

We have just mentioned the inadequacy of human intellect in solving the problem of man's nature and existence. Who is man? What is his destiny? Which direction should he choose in order

[1] Cf. Swami Prabhavananda, RP, p. 115.

to reach the goal? But answers to these riddles of existence itself are unknown to the normal range of human intellect. They must come from a realm beyond reason. There are two kinds of knowledge, says one Upaniṣad:

> To him then he said: 'There are two knowledges to be known — as indeed the knowers of Brahman are wont to say: a higher (*para*) and also a lower (*apara*).
> Of these, the lower is the Rig-Veda, the Yajur-Veda, the Sāma-Veda, the Atharva-Veda.
> Pronunciation, (*śikṣā*), Ritual (*kalpa*), Grammar, (*vyākaraṇa*), Definition (*nirukta*), Metrics (*chandas*), and Astrology (*jyotiṣa*).
> Now, the higher is that whereby that Imperishable (*akṣara*) is apprehended (MU 1.1.4-5).

The first is called lower knowledge, although it gives knowledge of the Vedas and other sciences. For it is still academic knowledge and entails distinction between the knower and the known. Even the knowledge of the scriptures is lower knowledge. But there is another knowledge, higher knowledge. It helps to gain knowledge of the Imperishable. It is perfect knowledge, different from logical thinking and realized as immediate perception of God. The one who gains this knowledge understands his being and destiny. The Īśa Upaniṣad which opens with the conception of God immanent in the universe (Īśa U 1), asks what delusion and what sorrow can afflict the one who has this knowledge:

> In whom all beings
> Have become just (*eva*) the Self of the discerner —
> Then what delusion (*moha*), what sorrow (*śoka*) is there
> Of him who perceives this unity! (Īśa U 7).

According to Advaita there are three faculties of the human mind which can be used for the attainment of truth: senses, reason and intuition — the Upaniṣadic equivalent of hearing, reflection and meditation (BU 2.4.5). Through senses man gathers knowledge of sense-objects. Reason functions on the conscious plane, but it must give way to intuition in which it finds fulfilment. Senses and intellect function within a limited sphere. They cannot guarantee the knowledge of God. The Kaṭha Upaniṣad teaches that they are less important than spiritual contemplation:

> Him who is hard to see, entered into the hidden,
> Set in the secret place [of the heart], dwelling in the depth, primeval —

By considering him as God, through the Yoga-study of what pertains
to self,
The wise man leaves joy and sorrow behind (KU 2.12).

The poverty of the intellect manifests itself when it confronts the Absolute. The Absolute of the Upaniṣads is not an object of ordinary knowledge. No one can claim to acquire Its knowledge. The Kena Upaniṣad 11 (3) teaches:

It is conceived of by him by whom It is not conceived of.
He by whom It is conceived of, knows It not.
It is not understood by those who [say they] understand It.
It is understood by those who [say they] understand It not.

The Absolute is not attained by the power of the intellect. Therefore if anyone thinks that he knows It, he does not, in reality, know It. It is not liable to philosophical investigations. In contrast, those who feel an intellectual humility realize It by becoming one with It. They realize It in meditation, when their reason melts away in pure intuition, says the Muṇḍaka Upaniṣad:

Not by sight is It grasped, not even by speech,
Not by any other sense-organs (*deva*), austerity, or work.
By the peace of knowledge (*jñāna-prasāda*), one's nature purified —
In that way, however, by meditating, one does behold Him who is
without parts (MU 3.1.8).

Thus it is intuitive awareness alone, obtained in meditation, which can discover the mystery of man and illumine his path toward God. In this illumination his whole being is uplifted towards a divine presence. He catches a glimpse of the truth of God. Perhaps he cannot understand or describe it. But he experiences it; he becomes new.

Here Swami Prabhavananda speaks of the 'beatific vision of the Absolute' and insists that every individual must experience it for himself. "... the revealed words of the scriptures are misunderstood if we are satisfied to accept them on mere authority rather than to try to discover their truth for ourselves." [2] He gives an illustration: It is one thing to hear about milk, another thing to see milk, and still another thing to taste milk.[3] To know the Absolute is to experience It. According to Swami Prabhavananda in

[2] *Ibid.,* p. 116.
[3] Cf. *ibid.*

the matter of inquiry into Brahman, one's own personal experience is the final proof.[4] The main principle of religion is realization, the experience of God.[5] The substance of religion is not in intellectual understanding but in being and becoming. It seems that his main concern is the ways and means for man to gain this experience. He explains himself:

> Religion to the Hindu is the direct experience of God, union with the Godhead. It is not enough to believe that God is; the living presence of God must be felt. Next, faith in that living presence must be transformed into the vision of God; the words of the scriptures must be transformed into vision. You must come directly and immediately into union with God. That is the definition of religion given in the Indian scriptures.[6]

One may read the sacred scriptures. One may also believe in them. But such understanding does not make one spiritual. What counts in spiritual life is an experience of God within oneself which characterizes his whole person. He cannot say that God is, until he has this unique spiritual experience.

But how to attain this spiritual experience? Swami Prabhavananda answers that the way is meditation:

> In order to know God, an inner vision needs to be awakened. The power of inner vision, the transcendental consciousness, is in every one of us. Only it lies dormant. It needs to be awakened. This awakening comes through loving worship of God and an unbroken communion with Him.[7]

This unbroken communion with God according to Swami Prabhavananda is meditation. It opens the inner vision of man's ultimate ground. "When we experience God, our life becomes transformed, our consciousness illumined." [8] This transformation of life and consciousness is the sign of an authentic spiritual life. The senses and the mind fail to reach God because He is not an object; He is the eternal subject. Yājñavalkya tells that the Self is Its own light when the sun has set, when the moon has set, when the fire has gone out and when the speech is hushed (BU 4.3.2-6). Therefore God

---

[4] Cf. *ibid.*

[5] Cf. *ibid.*, p. 128.

[6] Swami Prabhavananda, "Sri Ramakrishna and the Religion of Tomorrow," in: *Vedanta for Modern Man* (London, 1952), p. 130.

[7] Id., RP, p. 160.

[8] *Ibid.*, p. 159.

cannot be known in the way an empirical object is known. He is known only through a direct, immediate experience of Him.

All the attempts by the human intellect to define God will end in failure. The abstractions of the intellect need to be converted into the actuality of spiritual experience. Therefore silence is the best means to describe God. All that man can do is to cultivate a religious disposition. Yājñavalkya, the most prominent philosopher of the Upaniṣads, wanted to divide his property between his two wives, Kāthyāyanī and Maitreyī. The latter asked that if this whole earth filled with wealth were hers, would she be immortal thereby? 'No,' said Yājñavalkya. 'Your life would be just the same as the life of the rich. Regarding immortality, however, there is no hope through wealth.' Maitreyī renounced the riches of the world remarking, 'What should I do with that through which I may not be immortal?' The sage, seeing the spiritual disposition of his wife, imparted to her the highest knowledge (BU 2.4.1-3).

The way is clear. It is meditation. The aspirant should reorientate his inclinations, turning away from the outside world and looking within himself. He cannot hope for the interior spiritual experience, so long as he is lost in the outside world. He should select a place favourable for thought, restrain his mind and put an end to all desires. The mind should strip away its contents in complete detachment, regain its once dissipated potencies and fix its attention on God. Concentrated attention strengthens in a purified mind. A careful, systematic practice of ethical disciplines, a renewal of the mind, heart and will is required. The practice of meditation is to be persevered until the veil of truth is lifted.

2. *Meditation as the Constant Remembrance of God*

Swami Prabhavananda seems to lay stress on the idea of meditation as an unbroken memory of God.[9] God alone is to be worshipped day and night in and through every aspect of life without any distracting thought. This is a state to be achieved through the practice of spiritual disciplines. In this state there is constant recollectedness of God, the stream of the aspirant's loving thought flowing toward Him without any break or distraction. The unbroken stream of thought focused on God is likened to oil which is poured from one vessel to another in a continuous flow. When this kind

---

[9] Cf. *ibid.*, p. 138.

of remembrance is there, all bondages break. The spiritual eye opens, and the meditant sees God in everything. He lives in the bliss of God. Thus constant recollection is considered to be a means to liberation. This recollection is of the same nature as sight. He who is near can be seen; but he who is far can only be remembered. Nevertheless the above kind of remembering is as good as seeing. This remembrance, when practised constantly, assumes the same form as seeing.

When the mind thus runs in a steady stream toward God, the meditant attains supreme love and thereby reaches his union with God. For Kṛṣṇa says in the Gītā:

> Hear, O son of Pṛithā, how thou shallt without doubt know me fully, if thy mind be attached to me, if thou practise the method of work, if thou rely on me (BG 7.1).

Here Kṛṣṇa asks Arjuna to meditate on him as a means of concentrating his mind. Arjuna has to attach his mind to Kṛṣṇa, that is to say, surrender his whole personality to him. This is the means to know Kṛṣṇa in his fullness.

By constantly dwelling on the thought of God, the meditator leaves behind the empirical world. His mind becomes tranquil. The illustration given is of the unflickering flame of a lamp burning in a windless spot (BG 6.19). In the quiet of this mental state there is felt the presence of God in a very tangible manner. At the culmination, the meditator reaches the highest realization, an all-annihilating experience. The phenomenal world is totally effaced from his consciousness. Knowledge of God permeates his whole being. The ego disappears. All his desires melt away. He transcends the bound of empirical existence. He is absorbed in the bliss of Brahman. Like a drop in the ocean of Brahman, he becomes one with It. There is no more sorrow and grief. The Muṇḍaka Upaniṣad describes this experience as follows:

> The knot of the heart is loosened,
> All doubts are cut off,
> And one's deeds (*karman*) cease
> When He is seen — both the higher and the lower (MU 2.2.8).

In this way meditation, which is a constant remembrance of God, renders the seeker fit to gain the spiritual realization.

3. *Meditation as the Life in God*

In Swami Prabhavananda's view meditation is a life of absorption in God. A whole life is needed to unfold its meaning. Constant meditation, Swami Prabhavananda understands, is an attempt to unite our minds with Pure Consciousness, a flow of meditation on God, when in the mind there is absolutely nothing but God.[10] This method develops with practice. Keep the mind fixed on God. The ordinary man's mind wanders from one object to another, and at the time of meditation, too, various thoughts come up and dissipate its powers. Should any thought arise in the mind, the meditator must sit calmly and watch in which direction the mind tends to wander. By continuing to observe in this way, the mind becomes calm and dissociates itself from all thought-waves. Swami Prabhavananda asks for strenuous effort to concentrate the mind solely on God, in this manner.[11] When the thought of God and desire for Him become strong, the mind regains the power to resist all attachments to sense-objects.

This is a positive method. The negative method of trying to make the mind blank seldom or never succeeds. The positive approach consists in keeping the mind and heart on God, constantly and unceasingly. It is a stage of spiritual intimacy with God. The meditator feels that his life is actually encircled by the divine presence. On his part he has only to maintain the constant flow of thought toward God. When the mind is constantly united with God, it has reached a higher stage of meditation. Swami Prabhavananda terms it the state of constant recollectedness (*dhruva smṛti*).[12]

Persistent practice of meditation is the secret of success in spiritual life. The disciple should meditate in solitude. He should not give up this practice even if he does not always find peace or happiness in it. Here Swami Prabhavananda warns against a possible danger.[13] When the disciple begins to meditate, he often feels that he is getting worse rather than better. For a while it seems that his mind is more distracted and impure than before. This happens because the mind is stirred. There is no reason for depression. He has to continue struggling till he forms a regular habit of meditation. His mind gradually becomes calm and the thought of God completely

10 Cf. *ibid.*, pp. 145-146.
11 Cf. *ibid.*, p. 146.
12 Cf. *ibid.*
13 Cf. *ibid.*, p. 139.

fills his mind. God satisfies him entirely. He now knows that infinite happiness, which is a gift to those well versed in the sacred science, who are without crookedness and free from desire (BU 4.3. 33), is beyond the grasp of the senses. The Śvetāśvatara Upaniṣad encourages him with the assurance of gaining his purpose (SU 2. 11-13). As he practises meditation, he will visualize forms resembling fog, smoke, sun, fire, wind, fireflies, lightning, crystal and the moon. These are signs that he is on his way to the realization of God. When he becomes absorbed in meditation, he will be blessed with the vision of God Himself:

> Even as a mirror stained by dust
> Shines brilliantly when it has been cleansed,
> So the embodied one, on seeing the nature of the Soul (Ātman),
> Becomes unitary, his end attained, from sorrow freed.
> When with the nature of the self, as with a lamp,
> A practiser of Yoga beholds here the nature of Brahma,
> Unborn, steadfast, from every nature free —
> By knowing God (*deva*) one is released from all fetters!
> (SU 2.14-15)

This spiritual vision comes at the end of a life of meditation. It is like a fire which consumes all doubts concerning God. All his querries are stilled by the God-vision. What he intends to achieve through the constant practice of meditation is to centre his life in God. When, through spiritual disciplines, he becomes established in constant recollectedness of God, then alone is he convinced that he is actually in God's presence. It is through practice that he becomes immersed in the thought of God. As he thinks of Him more and more, constant recollectedness takes place. When he reaches this state he feels the presence of God continuously. Swami Prabhavananda speaks about the necessity of living in God's presence and directing the thoughts uninterruptedly toward Him. How it transforms spiritual life is made clear in his following words:

> Through the practice of these disciplines, constant recollectedness of God awakens in the devotee's heart. The thought of his beloved Lord is continually in his consciousness. All cravings leave him. Only one desire remains: to love God and live in complete self-surrender to his will. This pure and selfless devotion is followed by absorption in God, and ultimate union with him.[14]

---

[14] Swami Prabhavananda, *Sermon on the Mount,* p. 80.

This interpretation is evidently from the dualistic viewpoint. In the Advaitic realization of the Absolute, instead of constant recollectedness of God, there is an experience of oneness. As the knower becomes absorbed in meditation, he is said to realize that the Self is one with Brahman. It is similar to the experience when oil is poured into oil, water into water (KU 4.15), they blend into absolute oneness. But according to Swami Prabhavananda, both in the Advaitic and the dualistic concepts, this experience is the result of meditation. It is through the practice of the presence of God in the heart that the disciple takes his first step in meditation. It will also be his last step when he feels enveloped by the constant presence of God.

B. Swami Prabhavananda on Christian meditation

In chapter five we tried to present Swami Prabhavananda's understanding of Christian meditation. We analysed there the different elements of Christian meditation from his viewpoint. As an example of Christian meditation we presented his meditation on Christ and the Lord's Prayer, and saw that according to him, they contain the chief elements of Christian meditation.

Here our aim is quite limited. We do not intend to reexamine the same; we want only to see how Swami Prabhavananda uses Christian meditation in support of his ideas of meditation in Advaita.

Swami Prabhavananda is an avowed Advaitin. This does not mean that he depreciates other religions and philosophies; quite the opposite. His openness to other religions is praiseworthy. But he also takes pains to bring to light the Advaita ideals in other religions. This is quite evident when he interprets meditation. For example, when he interprets meditation according to Śrī Rāmānuja, he does it in such a way as to give the impression that Rāmānuja's views do not differ from his own.[15]

Now let us consider how he interprets meditation on Christ to suit his view. In his first spiritual experience of Christ he meditated on Him within and felt His living presence.[16] Commenting on *Yoga-sūtra* 1.37, he regards Christ as a holy personality and asks the yogi to meditate on the heart of Christ. The whole Hindu spirituality

[15] Cf. Swami Prabhavananda, SHI, pp. 313-314.
[16] Cf. Id., RP, p. 209.

has a predilection for the idea of the heart. Hinduism teaches that the heart, imagined to be a lotus bud, is the most appropriate place for divine meditation.[17] It is also called *Brahmapura,* the abode of Brahman. In the second meditation on Christ he approaches Him in the form of a chosen ideal.[18] As a follower of Śrī Rāmakṛṣṇa, he has no reservations to regard Christ as a chosen ideal and meditate on Him as such. But this is an Advaitic view, not Christian. He gives a third meditation on Christ.[19] It has three successive stages. First, Christ is meditated on merely as a human being. In the second place, He is meditated on as an *avatār.* Thirdly, when meditation on Christ deepens, it is the Absolute behind Christ that is meditated on. Christ is only a limited, partial representation of the Absolute. In all these instances Swami Prabhavananda means to say that meditation on Christ is not as sublime as the Advaita meditation on the formless Absolute.

Now turning to the meditation on the Lord's Prayer, in which he puts together the chief elements of Christian meditation, we notice the same Advaita influence in him. In addressing God as "Our Father," Christ, he thinks, teaches His disciples to enter the child-parent relationship as taught by the *bhakti* schools of Hindu mysticism. To be in heaven according to him is to enter into one's own consciousness and unfold the latent divinity.[20] Thus it means to him the realization of God in transcendental consciousness. The expression "hallowed be thy name" is according to him equivalent to the Hindu practice of repeating God's name. In the second part of the prayer, the petition to "forgive us our debts, as we also have forgiven our debtors," he interprets as the Hindu doctrine of *karma.*[21] And he introduces the theory of *māyā* in order to explain the petition "lead us not into temptation, but deliver us from evil."

In short, we think we may be justified in taking the conclusion that Swami Prabhavananda tries to read Advaita even in his interpretation of Christian meditation.[22]

---

[17] By means of various expressions the Upaniṣads teach that the heart is the spiritual centre in man. The chief expressions are the following: "lotus of the heart" cf. Maitrī U 6.2; "secret place of the heart" cf. KU 2.12; 3.1; 4.6; MU 2. 1.8; 3.1.7; TU 2.1.1; Maitrī U 6.4; "space within the heart" cf. BU 2.1.17; CU 3. 12.9; 8.1.1-3; BU 5.3 equates the heart with Brahman and Prajā-Pati.

[18] Cf. SWAMI PRABHAVANANDA on *Yoga-sūtra* I.48.

[19] Cf. *ibid.,* I.51.

[20] Cf. SWAMI PRABHAVANANDA, RP, p. 28.

[21] Cf. ID., *Sermon on the Mount,* pp. 94-95.

[22] We shall give here two statements by Swami Prabhavananda which show

C. What is Christian meditation?

Today a wave of meditation practice rises in the world. Some see this as one of the hopeful signs of the time. This movement has entered also the realm of Christianity, although it must be confessed that the impulse did not originate from within it. The growing awareness and desire for meditation within the Church is not out of curiosity, admitted that today the movement is not always associated with religion or spirituality. In this article we shall try to highlight some of the existential aspects of Christian meditation.

1. *Meditation as Experience*

Our time yearns for meditation. What is the reason for the spiritual vacuum felt today? Is not contemporary man lost in the world? How many people realize the meaning and fullness of life? How many come to their own true selves?

These are questions of prime importance. Man has the duty of realizing his full destiny, human and divine. It is a difficult task to become fully human, to come to the full realization of his supernatural destiny. For man lives today in an atmosphere hostile to this.[23]

---

how he interprets Christian meditation in terms of Advaita. They form part of his reflections upon Christ's saying "I and the Father are one" (Jn 10:30). He believes that this saying of Christ is the expression of a mystical experience and places it on the same level as the great saying "That thou art." He writes: "When the Upanishads declare 'Thou art That,' or when Christ says, 'I and my Father are one,' the actual experience is not conveyed because the sense of 'That' and 'thou,' of 'I' and 'Father' has returned." (Swami Prabhavananda, RP, p. 39). The following is a meditation on "I and the Father are one": "Consider yourself as a temple of God ... let your individual self be like a candle flame, and merge this flame in the great Light. Then there remains only the great Light, and you will find I and my Father are one." (Swami Prabhavananda, RP, p. 42). He concludes that this meditation, just as the meditation on "That thou art," effects the mystical union with God and the universe.

[23] Klemens Tilmann in his *Die Führung zur Meditation: Ein Werkbuch* I (Benziger Verlag, Zürich, Einsiedeln, Köln, 1974), pp. 17-21 explains four fundamentals:

1. Floating on the periphery. There is an increasing danger of leading life away from the inmost and what truly belongs to the person.

2. Long tension condition. The tendency to extroversion and unfulfilled desires create a tension condition in the human personality.

3. One-sided thinking. The ordinary way of knowledge is only one way of human knowledge. The meditative, intuitive, seeing-knowledge is often lacking.

4. The loss of the deep layers. The deep self is often forgotten; its place is taken by the peripheral ego. The depth of human personality is thus disregarded.

To be truly oneself demands therefore conscious effort. Every one knows only a part of his self; he does not know his being and aspirations perfectly; he does not see his end clearly. Indeed how many get to the depth of their being? It is only in the depth that man is capable of getting a glimpse of the mystery of human existence. Those who have never had this experience are unable to show their true character and intentions. They do not live; they are lived. Therefore in order to realize the meaning of being they need a renewal. How many realize their whole spiritual reality? Certainly very few.

In many ways people slip away from their real selves; often they do not realize their true selves at all. The peripheral ego dominating the true self, in which case people sometimes live in a split condition. The peripheral ego has only a superficial existence. He who is lost in this ego is lost to himself. And Jesus said: "He who loves his life loses it, and he who hates his life in this world will keep it for eternal life" (Jn 12:25). He who is subject to the selfish ego harms himself; he who controls it, wins his true self and rises to full life. A death of this ego is necessary in order to be able to live in the thought of God. For the selfish ego is wholly preoccupied with itself.

But how can one come to one's true self? The word 'self' points to a deep mystery which man carries within himself. It is the experience of what is underlying in him and in his relatedness to the world of man. But this experience has hitherto escaped his phenomenal existence. For this he must look at himself in a new light and grasp the meaning of being man, in himself, in his relation with other men and in his relation to the ground of his being, God. In other words, it is getting to his very self, entering the goal of his life, God, and in this sense he must again become man. Thus in his own being a man must find the meaning of his human existence and from there bring his life to fullness.[24]

In this process of becoming man meditation plays an important role.[25] It is a way to man's depth, for it takes place in the depth of the person. It brings about a transformation. The meditator begins to let truth enter him, take hold of him and transform him. He begins to experience freedom from the peripheral ego. He finds

---

[24] Cf. Karlfried Graf Dürckheim, *Meditieren - wozu und wie* (Herder, Freiburg, Basel, Wien, 1976), p. 17.

[25] Cf. Klemens Tilmann, *Die Führung zur Meditation*, p. 224.

the meaning of his existence. He accepts himself in a new breadth and depth. He experiences a development. This too takes a forward direction: from not-his-own to his-own; from peripheral to depth; from dispersion to recollection. He accepts responsibility, takes part in social groups and commits himself to work. In all these he experiences himself, finds himself and becomes himself. K. Tilmann employs the analogy of a tree.[26] To understand a tree it is necessary to understand the earth in which it is rooted, the place where it stands, light, air and the sun. So also we cannot know a human person until we know where he is finally rooted, and more, where he is on the way. While he is on the way, meditation helps him to become human and Christian. In short, man discovers God by discovering what he himself is. An experience is needed for this self-discovery, which meditation readily offers.

2. *Meditation as Faith-experience*

When we stress the point that meditation is a way to the depth of the human personality, resulting in experience, a very reasonable question may be raised: is the experience in meditation absolutely the same, regardless of the meditator's creed? Since the Christian has to build his life on faith and not on experience alone, he cannot by-pass his faith in pursuit of a meditative experience. Because, there can be experience in contraposition to the Christian faith. Therefore what is the relevance of meditation in a Christian context?

Our answer is that meditation has a religious orientation and for the Christian it is lived by faith. The Christian experiences God in the experience of his faith. Hence for a Christian the experience in meditation is unique: it is a faith-experience.

Under this aspect of faith-experience we may compare meditation to a way and the meditator to a wayfarer.[27] When a Christian begins the search for God in meditation, he undertakes a spiritual pilgrimage. Jesus said: "I am the way, and the truth, and the life; no one comes to the Father, but by me" (Jn 14:6). To follow Jesus was expressed in the early Church as belonging to the Way (Acts 9:2). In fact in Christianity 'the Way' is Jesus Himself. He has given us an example, by which we may follow

---

26 Cf. *ibid.*, p. 231.

27 Cf. JOSEPH SAUER, „Aspekte einer christlichen meditation," in: *Glaubenserfahrung und Meditation,* ed. Joseph Sauer (Herder, Freiburg, Basel, Wien, 1975), pp. 28-30.

in His steps (I Pt 2:21). Therefore Christ being the way, Christian meditation is also going 'the Way.' In going this way, it is faith that throws light on his path. Therefore the Christian's journey along the paths of meditation is a journey in the light of faith. In this light he walks securely and hopes to meet God at the end of the journey.

The light of faith is necessary at all stages of Christian meditation. It will extinguish only in the beatific vision, in the vision of God as He is, face to face (I Cor 13:12). The Christian has the assurance of this beatific vision, which is the crown for a life of faith in Christ as the fruit of His resurrection. The idea of the beatific vision consists in this, that the children of God gaze upon God and God gazes upon them; this is continuous, every moment revealing new dimensions in the vision of God. But while we are still on our journey, faith gives us a spiritual vision of what our intellect struggles to understand. For "God is more than the experience of God, than the knowledge of God, than the dogma of God." [28]

Therefore, while the meditator is on his way to God, he will at all moments need faith. It encourages him to take his first hesitant steps; it will also be his unerring guide in the journey throughout. It enables him to open himself and find the answer to the revealing Word of God. Thus it leads to deeper faith. The deeper his faith is, the richer are the experiences. This is the faith-experience in meditation. And meditation itself is the unfolding of such faith.

3. *Meditation as a Dialogue with God*

Above we have seen that meditation is a way to discover oneself by a genuine introversion.[29] But this is only one side of the truth. If it were only a way to self-discovery, the meditator would have been able only to sink into himself and find nothing but himself. Christian meditation has a broader significance. It is also an opening outwards in the sense that the meditator goes out of himself, making God the centre of his being.[30]

---

[28] JOSEF SUDBRACK, "The Challenge of Eastern Meditation," in: *Monastic Studies,* 12 (1976) 143.

[29] See above, pp. 144-145.

[30] Cf. HEINRICH DUMOULIN, *Östliche Meditation und Christliche Mystik* (Verlag Karl Alber, Freiburg-München, 1966), pp. 135-136.

The encounter with God in Christ is an important aspect of Christian meditation. This encounter takes place in the form of a dialogue.

Dialogue, if it is to be a real existential interpersonal relationship, can be thought of only between two persons. The idea of dialogue in meditation corresponds to the idea of God. Non-dualist Hinduism, which has sublime philosophical speculations about the ultimate ground of being, has come to the conclusion that the Absolute is an indescribable *It*. Hence the spiritual support and the centre of meditation is no person according to Advaita. This is not all: the human individual is finally to disappear in the Absolute. Therefore in the Advaita doctrine of the Absolute and the individual self, the concept of 'person' does not predominate. Quite the contrary is the Christian concept of God and the individual. Christian theology speaks of a Thou. The Absolute in Christianity is a person, the one God in three persons. When this personal God offers man the mystery of salvation, and man responds to it positively, he is addressed as a person and raised to the fullness of his self, as a person. In this sense, Christian meditation is by no means the Advaitic identification of the Absolute and the individual; rather, it is the entry into the partnership between the finite personal man and the infinite personal God.

Christian meditation is essentially a personal event, resulting in an essential relationship to God. In meditation man communes with God as with a concrete Thou. We can speak of Thou only in an encounter. When the Thou is a person, the encounter assumes the form of a dialogue. In dialogue two persons feel to belong together. It is Christ who revealed the great mystery of divine-human relationship. God speaks to man, and man is allowed to speak to Him. In this encounter there is a personal dialogue. In it the I-Thou meet. God meets man freely, intently and with love and understanding.

The assurance of the possibility of this dialogue is given in revelation. Christian meditation unfolds itself essentially before the revealing Word of God. In revelation the Christian knows that his life is hidden in God and that his life is a sharing in the divine life of the Trinity. This is a great mystery according to St. Paul:

> O the depth of the riches and wisdom and knowledge of God! How unsearchable are his judgements and how unscrutable his ways!
> "For who has known the mind of the Lord,
> or who has been his counsellor?" (Rm 11:33-34)

It is again the mystery of God that He creates man in His image and likeness. He lifts him up to the participation of His divine nature (2 Pt 1:4). The Christian has also the promise "... we will come to him and make our home with him" (Jn 14:23). The Christian can meditate on this mystery, the fullness of the life given to him.

In Christ and through Him, man enters the world of divine life. Christ is the prototype and ideal of man's encounter with God. In Him, God makes accessible to man His divine life. In Christ, God offers man a new participation in His inner life. Christ in turn communicates His life to man and opens up to him infinite horizons on God. In following Christ, the Christian adheres to God, and lives from and in Him. Christ becomes the centre of his life in God.[31]

It belongs to the fundamental Christian existence to be "in Christ." Christ is the source of Christian meditation. For it takes place through His saving grace; and it ends through Him with Father and Holy Spirit. A Christian can meditate because he is in Christ. Christ is present to him not only as an outside guide, but through His Spirit given to him He is even within him.

Christ is not only the source of Christian meditation, but its content and goal as well. He is the image of the invisible God and the first-born of all creation (Col 1:19). Christ who became man is also the crucified one. He "emptied himself, taking the form of a servant, being born in the likeness of men. And being found in human form he humbled himself and became obedient unto death, even death on the cross" (Phil 2:7-8). But this God-become-man, this God crucified is also the risen Lord. Christian meditation also moves in this triple order. The entry into the one great Christ-mystery enkindles true meditation. The meditator tries to repeat the Christ-mystery in himself. He is indeed possessed by it. In Christ he becomes transparent. He experiences Christ in all and all in Christ (Col 3:11).

The dialogical aspect of meditation is continued through the Holy Spirit. The Christian has the promise of the continued assistance of Christ's Spirit. He is given the Holy Spirit. "... God's love has been poured into our hearts through the Holy Spirit who has been given us" (Rm 5:5). He lives in us. He leads us to the truth

[31] Cf. JOSEF SUDBRACK, *Meditation: Theorie und Praxis* (Echter Verlag Katholisches Bibelwerk, Würzburg, 1971), p. 95.

(Jn 16:13) and opens us to the gift of God and self for we are born of Him (Jn 3:8). The Spirit comes to us, takes us, overpowers us and transforms us. Thus He is our teacher of meditation. He gives us the power to pray. He enkindles meditation in us. We can go into the depth of the mystery of God in so far as we are led by the Spirit (I Cor 2:10-13). The Holy Spirit lifts us to a supernatural realm where we are able to meditate.

We have been examining the Trinitarian aspect of dialogue in meditation. This dialogue continues in the life of the Church. The sacraments of the Church, especially Baptism and Eucharist, make the mystery of Christ present in the life of the Christian. This life finds expression in the community of the faithful. For Christian meditation reaches its perfection in the communion of love.

D. A Christian integration of Hindu meditation

The demand for meditation within Christianity has never been so great as at present. Some think that it is only the rediscovery of a lost treasure. But it would be wrong to think that Christianity has never before seriously engaged in meditation. The fact is that Christianity has a rich tradition of meditation. It seems that the Gospels do not separate meditation from prayer. That is perhaps a reason why they report on Jesus' forty days in the wilderness and the nights spent in prayer without specific reference to His meditation. Luke's account "But Mary kept all these things, pondering them in her heart" (Lk 2:19) seems to indicate that Mary is the symbol of New Testament meditation. The tradition of Christian meditation encompasses also the two year life of St. Paul in the Arabian desert, the contemplative life of the Desert Fathers, the spiritual writings during the Middle Ages, the Spiritual Exercises of St. Ignatius Loyola, the mystical teachings of St. John of the Cross, Teresa of Avila and the monks on Mount Athos.

In this way the history of Christian spirituality has always been associated with meditation. Unfortunately this rich tradition has lost its vigour. In the early Church theology was not isolated from prayer and meditation. But after the Reformation it began to be thought of as an intellectual pursuit. Not even the theology of spiritual life was spared this approach. Unfortunately, this was detrimental to the meditative experience in Christianity.[32]

The situation remained unchanged for a very long time. Recently Hinduism and Buddhism have given Christianity the impetus to revitalize its old tradition. Granting that today not all people practise meditation with a religious motive, we limit our observations to those Christians who are psychologically sound and honestly religious, yet feeling some kind of uncertainty about their spiritual life. They doubt whether the traditional ways of Christian meditation could cope with their aspirations.[33] Therefore they seek it outside the Church. People then ask: is not the Church's duty to give her children the means to live their faith? Does this search for it in other religions mean a farewell to the Church?

We do not think that the Christian faith forbids us to learn what is good and noble from outside the Church. A Christian must be ready to accept what is true and holy in other religions. It is no humiliation. He could profit from the different forms and methods of meditation offered by other religions.

Here the Indian Christian experience has an important task. A closer understanding of Hindu meditation could enrich Christian spirituality. If Christianity has borrowed from Greek philosophy, why should it hesitate to do the same also with regard to Hinduism? Meditation is one of the most precious contents of Hindu spirituality. An Indian Christian spirituality cannot discard its salient features. But so far little or nothing is being done in this regard.[34]

We have chosen the theme of this study with the hope of arriving at a closer understanding of Hindu meditation. But since

---

[32] Cf. ERNS BENZ, „Meditation in östlichen Religionen und in Christentum," in: Ladislaus Boros, et al., *Bewußtseinserweiterung durch Meditation* (Herder, Freiburg, 1973), p. 94.

[33] By the traditional practice of meditation we mean the form of meditation used even today, beginning with a prayer, reading a text and reflecting on its mystery. This is not all that can be said about meditation. There are many methods of it, like the 'lectio sacra,' the meaningful reading of a text, practised by the monks in the Middle Ages. This method has a short-coming. It extols the role of the intellect. The whole man, with his psycho-somatic needs, is not fully considered.

[34] We may mention here the attempts made by the Benedictines in India. But even the Benedictine monk J.-M. Déchanet's *La Voie du Silence* (Desclée de Brouwer, Paris, 1956 = E.T. *Christian Yoga,* New York, 1972) is only a manual for Yoga exercises. Worth mentioning are the contributions to Indian way of monasticism and prayer by Swami Abhishiktananda. Recently M. Dhavamony has made some significant study on the theory of Hindu meditation in a series of articles. See sections II and IV of the bibliography at the end.

we limited our study of Hindu meditation to the interpretation of Swami Prabhavananda, an Advaitin, our study has not been able to bring out all the nuances of Hindu meditation as a whole. The meditation as interpreted by him is predominently Advaitic in character. Yet the study itself has revealed that there are common points between Hindu and Christian theology of meditation. Here, we may point out some common elements, as well as some essential differences, in both approaches that have come to the fore as a result of this study.

We have seen that the most significant meaning of meditation according to Swami Prabhavananda is that it is a way to the experience of God. We have also seen how in Christianity meditation is seen as an experience, and much more, as a faith-experience. Therefore the idea of experience is common to both traditions, although the content of this experience is not the same.

The idea of dialogue, an important aspect of Christian meditation, is absent in the Hindu concept of meditation. This, we think, is because of the difference in the concepts of 'person.' Dialogue can take place only between two persons. Since in non-dualist Hinduism the Absolute is supra-personal, It cannot be a partner in a dialogue. Quite different is the Christian viewpoint. In Christian theology God is personal in the sense that He is "Persons," not just one Person but three. This is the doctrine of the Holy Trinity. In the Christian idea of meditation, Christ invites us to enter into dialogue with Him and through Him with the Holy Trinity. Christ, the Son of God, wants us to be God's sons in the Son. To the extent that we reach this union with God, we become adopted sons of God and personalize ourselves in the manner of the Divine Persons. It is only at this juncture that we become truly persons.

Chapter two of this study was on the forms of meditation. There we discussed the loving meditation.[35] This form of meditation is similar to Christian meditation. The forms of love as described by Swami Prabhavananda approach the Christian idea of divine love. Success in loving meditation depends upon the intensity of love towards the chosen ideal. Swami Prabhavananda has in many places described Christ as a chosen ideal. The question of the place of Jesus Christ is central in Christian meditation. For He is, in Himself, the human and the divine united. That is why Christian theo-

---

[35] See above, pp. 44-48.

logians combine meditation of Christ with imitation of Christ. The meditator encounters God in Christ. The pattern of Jesus Christ has therefore a different meaning in Christian meditation than the doctrine of chosen ideal has in Hinduism. The Reality of Jesus Christ in itself represents the union of humanity and divinity and the faithful commune with God through Him. However, using Swami Prabhavananda's interpretation of loving meditation as a basis, Christian theology may develop a new form of meditation on Christ.

But according to Swami Prabhavananda loving meditation is not the highest form of meditation. For love, even when directed to God, remains on the emotional and dualistic level. As an Advaitin he prefers to be a knower. But Christianity, which has defined that God is love, teaches that real knowledge of God is also love of God. In this way it surpasses the seeming conflict between knowledge and love of God.

The highest form of meditation according to Swami Prabhavananda is meditation on the formless Absolute. We agree with him that the concept of the Absolute, the supra-personal, is a high attainment of human intellect within the Advaitic perspective of Being. But the idea of transcendence and immanence of God converge in a single person, Jesus Christ. Hence Christian meditation always has a goal: it is the vision of God, the beatific vision. The object of this vision and experience is not an inexplicable transcendent 'Nothing,' but the personal God. In this the Christian experiences his ultimate ground of being as having a personal significance.

But from another standpoint, a Christian may appreciate Swami Prabhavananda's explanation of meditation on the formless Absolute. Granting that the pattern of Jesus Christ has special meaning in Christian meditation, we think that some kind of objectless meditation is not unfamiliar to Christianity. There is a non-formalized, non-verbalized and non-conceptualized awareness of God within Christian meditation itself. Beyond the form of God there is deeply felt, a simple presence of God. In a highly elevated meditative mood the Christian meditator experiences his life and being as engulfed by the presence of God absolutley beyond any form. This experience penetrates into his very existence. His meditation is no more in the form of thought; it becomes a communion of love. This aspect of objectless meditation in Christianity is, we think, in line with Swami Prabhavananda's understanding of meditation on the formless Absolute which is one of his most meritorious contributions to Christian meditation.

Regarding the forms of meditation, the Christian has a variety of options. He may use all the forms and methods of Hindu meditation. Every method of Hindu meditation has come down to the present generation verified by the sages. Indian Christians should beware of the temptation to disparage the Hindu methods of meditation. They should be grateful to the spiritual heritage of India for this treasure of immense possibilities for meditation. All these possibilities could contribute to an increase of Christian religious experience. But the Christian must never forget that every method also has its dangers. We find people who follow no particular method of meditation but are absorbed in the thought of God all the same. In fact each Christian has to discover his own interior path in his journey toward God.

Finally, we come to the question of techniques of meditation. The conditions of the techniques are similar both in Hinduism and Christianity. Techniques connected with the position of the body, control of mind, conditions of concentration and meditation are similar. Hinduism has developed them praiseworthily. We should not label them as merely human techniques, having nothing spiritual about them. As a result of this study, we saw that they form part of an asceticism. Here we may find another chief contribution of Swami Prabhavananda to Christian meditation. His treatment of the meditation techniques shows that the Hindu meditator tries through them to attain an equanimity of the mind. The Christian too needs a tranquillity of spirit during his meditation. The techniques of meditation make the human spirit tranquil before God and show it the way to deeper experience of God. Using the techniques, a Christian may be able to intensify his experience of Christ. Even here he should not forget that the Hindu techniques of meditation are bound up with the Hindu concept of God, man and the universe. To the extent that the Christian can agree with the Hindu doctrine, he may accept them. Where he cannot accept it, he must separate the techniques of meditation from the doctrine peculiar to Hindu theology and may adapt them to Christian meditation. In so doing Christian theology is inflicting no violence on Hindu meditation techniques themselves. Nor is the fear justified, that the techniques would be deprived of their vitality when separated from their matrix. We have the example of Swami Prabhavananda himself, who although an Advaitin, has successfully grafted the techniques of Patañjali's Yoga meditation onto the Advaitic meditation on the formless Absolute. Moreover we think that this is, perhaps, the privilege of Indian Christian spirituality: to let the Hindu meditation techniques reach their Christian spiritual vision.

Now that we have examined the question of integrating a Christian way of Hindu meditation, we can return to those ideas on which we do not agree with Swami Prabhavananda's interpretation of meditation. Specifically we stress three main points of difference: (1) as regards Christian faith, the goal and content of Christian meditation are different from what he puts forward; (2) as regards Christian meditation, he lacks a clear understanding of it and interprets it in the light of Advaita; he changes the Christian idea in order to emphasize the superiority of his own view; (3) as regards his teaching itself, he associates meditation with knowledge, while the Christian associates it with love; knowledge as salvation reminds the Christian of the unpleasant consequences of Gnostic knowledge in the history of Christian theology.

We conclude with the hope that our study of meditation as a path to God-realization has indicated something, with regard to the many elements of Hindu meditation, that can be adopted by Christianity. Could Hindu meditation offer something positive to fill the spiritual vacuum created by the diminishing of meditative element in the Church? To answer the question, the first thing to do is to enter into a dialogue with Hinduism. We believe that the idea of meditation is a good meeting-point for a Hindu-Christian dialogue.

BIBLIOGRAPHY
A SELECT BIBLIOGRAPHY OF WORKS CONSULTED

I. Works by Swami Prabhavananda

A. *Original Works*

PRABHAVANANDA, Swami. *Vedic Religion and Philosophy.* Sri Ramakrishna Math, Madras, 1950[5].

———. *Religion in Practice.* George Allen & Unwin, London, 1968.

———. *Swami Premananda: Teachings and Reminiscences.* Vedanta Press, California, 1968.

———. *The Spiritual Heritage of India: A Comprehensive Exposition of Indian Philosophy and Religion.* Vedanta Press, California, 1969 (Second Paperback ed. First published 1963).

———. *The Eternal Companion: Spiritual Teachings of Swami Brahmananda.* Sri Ramakrishna Math, Madras, 1971[5].

———. *Yoga and Mysticism.* Vedanta Press, California, 1972.

———. *The Sermon on the Mount according to Vedanta.* Mentor Book, New York, 1972.

B. *Translations and Commentaries*

PRABHAVANANDA, Swami. tr., *The Upanishads: Breath of the Eternal.* Mentor Book, New York, 1957.

———. and JOHNSON, C. eds., *Prayers and Meditation: Compiled from the Scriptures of India.* Vedanta Press, California, 1967.

———. tr., *The Wisdom of God: Srimad Bhagavatam.* New York, 1968.

———. and ISHERWOOD, C. trs., *The Song of God: Bhagavad-Gita.* Sri Ramakrishna Math, Madras, 1969.

———. tr., *How to Know God: The Yoga Aphorisms of Patanjali.* Mentor Book, New York, 1969.

———. and ISHERWOOD, C. trs., *Shankara's Crest-Jewel* of *Discrimination (Viveka Chudamani) with a Garland of Questions and Answers (Prasnottara Malika).* Mentor Book, New York, 1970.

———. tr., *Narada's Way of Divine Love: The Bhakti Sutras.* Vedanta Press, California, 1971.

II. Hindu Spirituality and Meditation

The Cultural Heritage of India. I: *Early Phases.* II. *Itihāsas, Purāṇas, Dharma and other Śāstras.* III: *The Philosophies.* IV: *The Religions.* 4 vols published by Sri Ramakrishna Centenary Committee, Calcutta, 1953-1962; reprint 1969-1970.

DASGUPTA, Surendranath. *The Study of Patañjali.* University of Calcutta, 1920.

———. *Yoga Philosophy in Relation to other Systems of Indian Thought.* University of Calcutta, 1930.

DEUSSEN, Paul. *The System of Vedānta: According to Bādarāyaṇa's Brahma-Sūtras and Śaṁkara's Commentary.* Trans. Charles Johnston, Delhi, 1972 = First ed. Chicago, 1912.

DHAVAMONY, Mariasusai. "The Religious Quest of Hinduism," in: *Studia Missionalia,* 15 (1966) 65-82.

———. "Hindu Meditation," in: *Studia Missionalia,* 25 (1976) 115-165.

———. "Transcendental Meditation," in: *Secretariatus pro non christianis Bulletin,* XII/3 (1977) 154-167.

ELIADE, Mircea. *Le Yoga: Immortalité et Liberté.* Payot, Paris, 1954.

HILL, W. Douglas P. *The Bhagavadgītā.* E.T. and commentary. Second abridged ed. Oxford University Press, 1953.

HUME, Robert E., *The Thirteen Principal Upanishads.* Trans. from the Sanskrit. Second revised ed. Oxford University Press, 1931².

ISHERWOOD, Christopher. ed., *Vedanta for the Western World.* London, 1951 = First published 1948.

———. ed., *Vedanta for Modern Man.* London, 1952.

'M', *The Gospel of Sri Ramakrishna.* Originally recorded in Bengali by Mahendranath Gupta, trans. Swami Nikhilananda. Sri Ramakrishna Math, Madras, 1974⁶.

Meditation. Published by the Monks of the Ramakrishna Order. Ramakrishna Vedanta Centre, London, 1972.

NIKHILANANDA, Swami. *Self-Knowledge.* E.T. of Śaṁkara's *Ātmabodha* with Notes, Comments and Introduction. Sri Ramakrishna Math, Madras, 1947.

———. tr., *Vedāntasara of Sadānanda.* Advaita Ashrama, Calcutta, 1968.

RADHAKRISHNAN, S. *The Brahma Sūtra: The Philosophy of Spiritual Life.* Translation with an Introduction and Notes. George Allen & Unwin, London, 1960.

———. *The Principal Upaniṣads.* Ed. with Introduction, Text, Translation and Notes. George Allen & Unwin, London, 1974 = First published 1953.

ŚAṀKARA, Śrī. *Manīṣa-Pañcakam.* E.T. = *The Wisdom of Unity.* Trans. T.M.P. Mahadevan. Madras, 1967.

———. *Vākyavritti and Ātmajñānopadeśavidhi.* Trans. with explanatory Notes. Swami Jagadahanda. Madras, 1967.

———. *Pañcīkaraṇam.* Text and Varttika with word-for-word Translation, Comments and Glossary. Advaita Ashrama, Calcutta, 1972².

———. *Aparokṣānubhūti.* Text with word-for-word Translation and Notes. Swami Vimuktananda. Advaita Ashrama, Calcutta, 1973.

SATPRAKASHANANDA, Swami. *Methods of Knowledge according to Advaita.* George Allen & Unwin, London, 1965.

SIDDHESWARANANDA, Swami. "La Technique Hindoue de la Méditation," in:

Technique et Contemplation. Les Études Carmélitaines, Desclée de Brouwer, Paris, 1949, pp. 17-35.

———. *La Méditation selon le Yoga-Vedānta.* Paris, 1966.

THIBAUT, George. tr., *The Vedānta-Sūtras with the Commentary of Rāmānuja.* Vol. XLVIII of *The Sacred Books of the East,* ed. F. Max Müller, Oxford, 1904.

———. tr., *The Vedānta-Sūtras of Bādarāyana with the Commentary by Śaṅkara.* In two parts. Dover Publications, New York, 1962.

VIJÑĀNABHIKṢU. *Yogasāra-saṁgraha.* E. T. with Sanskrit Text. Trans. Ganganatha Jha. Bombay, 1894.

Viṣṇu Purāṇa. Trans. Horace Hayman Wilson. Calcutta, 1961^3 = First ed. London, 1840.

VIVEKANANDA, Swami. *Meditation and Its Methods.* Ed. Swami Chetanananda. Vedanta Press, California, 1976.

WARRIER, Krishna. *The Concept of Mukti in Advaita Vedānta.* Madras University Philosophical Series No. 9, 1961.

WOODS, James Haughton. *The Yoga-System of Patañjali.* Harward Oriental Series Vol. XVII. The Harward University Press, 1927.

ZAEHNER, Robert Charles. *The Bhagavad-Gītā: With a Commentary based on the Original Sources.* Oxford University Press, 1969 = Reprint 1976.

III. CHRISTIAN MEDITATION

BOROS, Ladislaus. hrsg., *Bewußtseinserweiterung durch Meditation.* Herder, Freiburg, 1973.

The Cloud of Unknowing. By an English Mystic of the Fourteenth Century. Ed. Dom Justin McCann. London, 1936 = First ed. 1924.

DÜRCKHEIM, Karlfried G. *Meditieren - Wozu und Wie.* Herder, Freiburg, 1976.

ENOMIYA-LASSALE, Hugo M. *Meditation als Weg zur Gotteserfahrung.* Köln, 1972.

The Holy Bible. Revised Standard Version: Catholic Edition, 1966.

LOTZ, Johannes B., *Kurze Anleitung zum Meditieren.* Knecht Verlag, Frankfurt a.M., 1973.

MELZER, Friso. *Konzentration Meditation Kontemplation.* Johannes Stauda Verlag, Kassel, 1974.

RAGUIN, Yves. *Chemins de la contemplation.* Desclée de Brouwer, Paris, 1969. E. T. = *Paths to Contemplation,* trans. Paul Barrett and ed. Edward Malatesta. Wheathampstead, Hertfordshire, 1975.

RAVIER, André. „Die ignatianische Kontemplation," in: *Internationale Katholische Zeitschrift,* 3 (1975) 228-233.

SAUER, Joseph. hrsg., *Glaubenserfahrung und Meditation: Wege einer neuen Spiritualität.* Herder, Freiburg, 1975.

SUDBRACK, Josef. *Meditation: Theorie und Praxis.* Echter Verlag, Würzburg, 1971^2.

———. „Meditation aus christlicher Tradition," in: *Stimmen der Zeit,* 11 (1972) 325-332.

———. *Meditation des Wortes: Hinführung und Einübung.* Echter Verlag, Würzburg, 1974.

TILMANN, Klemens. *Die Führung zur Meditation: Ein Werkbuch* I. Benziger Verlag, Zürich, 1974[6].

———. *Leben aus der Tiefe.* Kleine Anleitung zur inneren Versenkung und christlichen Meditation. Benziger Verlag, Zürich, 1975.

IV. HINDU-CHRISTIAN MEDITATION

ABHISHIKTANANDA, Swami. *La Rencontre de l'Hinduoisme et du Christianisme.* Paris, 1965. E. T. = *Hindu-Christian Meeting Point within the Cave of the Heart.* Trans. Sara Grant. Bombay, 1969.

———. "Yoga and Christian Prayer," in: *The Clergy Monthly,* XXXV (1971) 472-477.

———. *Prayer.* London, 1974[3].

BHAJANANANDA, Swami. "Hindu Upasana vis-à-vis Christian Meditation," in: *Journal of Dharma,* 2 (1977) 217-230.

Christian Monks and Asian Religions (*In collaboration*): Proceedings of the Second Asian Monastic Congress. Bangalore, October 14-22, 1973, in: *Cistercian Studies,* IX (1974: 2 & 3) 90-211.

CUTTAT, Jacques-Albert. "Expérience Chrétienne et Spiritualité Orientale," in: *La Mystique et les Mystiques,* ed. A. Ravier. Paris, 1965, pp. 825-1020.

DÉCHANET, J.-M., *La Voie du Silence.* Paris, 1956. E. T. = *Christian Yoga,* trans. R. Hindmarsh. New York, 1960.

———. *Yoga and God.* Search Press, London, 1974.

DHAVAMONY, Mariasusai. "Christian Experience and Hindu Spirituality," in: *Gregorianum,* 48 (1967) 776-791.

———. "Hindu Meditation and Christian Evaluation of It," in: *Secretariatus pro non christianis Bulletin,* 23-24 (1973) 103-116.

DUMOULIN, Heinrich. *Östliche Meditation und Christliche Mystik.* Karl Alber Verlag, Freiburg/München, 1966.

GRIFFITHS, Bede. "Indian Christian Contemplation," in: *The Clergy Monthly,* XXXV (1971) 277-281.

MONCHANIN, Jules. *Mystique de l'Inde, mystère chrétien.* Ecrits et inédits. Présentés par Suzanne Siauve, avant-propos de Pierre Fallon. Fayard, Paris, 1974.

NEUNER, Josef. „Östliche und Christliche Meditation," in: *Geist und Leben,* 6 (1974) 408-421.

SUDBRACK, Josef. "The Challenge of Eastern Meditation," in: *Monastic Studies,* 12 (1976) 121-150.

WALDENFELS, Hans. *Meditation - Ost und West.* Benziger Verlag, Zürich, 1975.

V. GENERAL STUDIES ON HINDUISM

CHATTERJEE, Satischandra. *The Fundamentals of Hinduism: A Philosophical Study.* Calcutta, 1950.

GONDA, Jan. *Les Religions de l'Inde.* 3 tomes. Payot, Paris, 1962-1966.
———. *Change and Continuity in Indian Religion.* London, 1965.
HIRIYANNA, M. *Outlines of Indian Philosophy.* George Allen & Unwin, London, 1970[8] = First Published 1932.
KEITH, Arthur B. *The Religion and Philosophy of the Veda and Upanishads.* 2 vols. The Harward Oriental Series Vols. XXXI-XXXII. Cambridge, 1925.
MORGAN, Kenneth W., ed. *The Religion of the Hindus.* New York, 1953.
OLDENBERG, Herman. *Die Religion des Veda.* Stuttgart und Berlin, 1917[2].
———. *Die Lehre der Upanishaden und die Anfänge des Buddhismus.* Göttingen, 1923[2].
RENOU, Louis. *Religions of Ancient India.* Jordan Lectures in Comparative Religion 1951. University of London, 1953.
SHARMA, D. S. *Hinduism Through the Ages.* Bharatiya Vidya Bhavan Bombay, 1973.
ZAEHNER, Robert Charles. *Hinduism.* Oxford University Press, London, 1962.

DOCUMENTA MISSIONALIA

Documenta Missionalia is a collection of scholarly studies on missionary, anthropological and cultural aspects of non-Christian peoples related to their religious, historical and ethnological contexts, published by the Faculty of Missiology of the Gregorian University.

I. - Jesús LOPEZ-GAY, S. J. - *El matrimonio de los japoneses.* (Problema y soluciones según un ms. inédito de Gil de la Mata [1547-1599]). 1964. pp. 185.

II. - Jesús LOPEZ-GAY, S. J. - *El catecumenado en la misión del Japón del siglo XVI.* 1966. pp. VIII-252.

III. - Vincenzo M. POGGI, S. J. - *Un classico della spiritualità musulmana.* 1967. pp. XII-279.

IV. - Jesús LOPEZ-GAY, S. J. - *La liturgia en la Misión del Japón del siglo XVI.* 1970. pp. VIII-329.

V. - Mariasusai DHAVAMONY, S. J. (Editor) - *Evangelization, Dialogue and Development.* 1972. pp. VIII-358.

VI. - Marcel ZAGO, OMI - *Rites et cérémonies en milieu bouddhiste Lao.* 1972. pp. X-408.

VII. - Mariasusai DHAVAMONY, S. J. - *Phenomenology of Religion.* 1973. pp. XI-335.

VIII. - Ary A. ROEST CROLLIUS, S. J. - *The Word in the Experience of Revelation in Qur'ān and Hindu Scriptures.* 1974. pp. XVI-273.

IX. - Mariasusai DHAVAMONY, S. J. (Editor) - *Evangelization.* 1975. pp. XVI-404.

X. - Giuseppe PIRAS - *La Congregazione e il Collegio di Propaganda Fide di J. B. Vives, G. Leonardi e M. De Funes.* 1976. pp. XI-154.

XI. - Gianfranco COFFELE, SDB. - *Johannes Christiaan Hoekendijk: da una teologia della missione ad una teologia missionaria.* 1976. pp. 550.

UNIVERSITA' GREGORIANA EDITRICE

Piazza della Pilotta, 4 - 00187 Roma (Italy)